THIS IS RIDICULOUS
THIS IS AMAZING

THIS IS RIDICULOUS

THIS IS AMAZING

PARENTHOOD IN 71 LISTS

JASON GOOD, Family Man

CHRONICLE BOOKS
San Francisco

To Lindsay, Silas, and Arlo

Library of Congress Cataloging-in-Publication Data:
Good, Jason.
  This is ridiculous this is amazing : parenthood in 71 lists / Jason Good.
    pages cm
  ISBN 978-1-4521-2921-1 (hardback)
1. Child rearing—Humor. 2. Parent and child—Humor. I. Title.

  PN6231.C315G73 2014
  649'.10207—dc23
          2013032528

Manufactured in China

MIX
Paper from
responsible sources
FSC® C008047

Cover designed by Jennifer Tolo Pierce
Author photo by Ben Toht

Book designed by Benjamin Shaykin
Typeset mostly in Sentinel,
Atlas Grotesk, and Router.

10 9 8 7 6 5 4 3 2 1

Chronicle Books LLC
680 Second Street
San Francisco, California 94107
www.chroniclebooks.com

Contents

Acknowledgments*

My editor, Lorena Jones at Chronicle,
who believed I could write a book.

My agent, Courtney Miller-Calihan,
who has held my hand for longer than
she might have liked.

My wife, Lindsay Forsythe,
who made this book funnier and
made me happier.

My parents, Michael and Josephine Good,
who taught me by example
to see the humor in everyday life.

My sons, Silas and Arlo,
who created all of the content in this book,
and somehow managed
to fill me with joy in the process.

*These acknowledgments serve as payment for all debts.

Introduction

DO YOU HAVE AN ABRASION CAUSED BY A TODDLER hitting you with a tambourine, harmonica, or random piece of cardboard?

Have you used a baby wipe to clean yogurt off your "comfy pants"?

Are your remote controls mysteriously greasy?

If you answered "Yes," or "Please help me" to any of these questions, I wrote this book for you.

Of course, I realize that, as a parent, obtaining or reading a book might prove difficult. Sure, they're available for immediate download, but your Page Genie, Book Horse, Text Sniffer, Word Wrangler, etc., were all co-opted by your kid months ago. So someone probably gave you this book while saying something like, "This made me think of you," or "Wow, you smell tired." The good news: This is a book of lists (seventy-one of them, in fact—one for each gray hair you've found since having children), so the introduction here is the only heavy reading you'll have to do.

If you're in a store right now skimming this and thinking it might be a great gift for your gal pal who carried around a breast pump, or your guy friend whose wife carried around a breast pump, or your guy friend who carried around his wife's breast pump, or even your friend who got drunk and bought a breast pump as a gag, you're right, it is.

I wrote this book because I like making people laugh. I'm a stand-up comedian, but parenting has made me lazy with my downtime, and writing involves a lot of sitting. I would have written a regular book full of sentences and ideas, but being the father of two young boys has caused my IQ to plummet. The relentless emotional negotiations between love, frustration, and guilt kill more brain cells than huffing patio sealant. I would love to write a hilarious thingy about string theory (lie), but considering I'm frequently incapable of untwisting the strap on a car seat, it's probably best for the universe if I leave science-y stuff to the experts.

It's also worth acknowledging that some parents are perfect. Their kids sleep through the night, they never watch TV, they "super love" lettuce, they never pick their nose, they don't bite people, and they pronounce the *L* in *clock*. I didn't write this for them. They wouldn't have time to read it anyway because they're probably off in a pasture reading Shakespeare to an infant. I'm happy for them. This book is for the rest of us, or anyone else who enjoys laughing at the irony of being so helplessly in love with tiny people who have no idea that they're slowly killing us.

PREPAREDNESS

The mere suggestion that one can be prepared for parenthood is preposterous, but there are a few things you should know. Let me be clear: None of this advice will make your ridiculous life any easier, but at least you won't feel alone (or wind up needing your retina reattached).

How to Defend Yourself Against a Toddler Attack

Let's start with something very dear to my heart: personal safety. It's important to understand that your children are completely unaware, or perhaps simply don't care, that they're capable of injuring you severely. I like that my small son thinks I'm indestructible, but at the same time, I don't appreciate having my mouth pried open like a begrudging dental patient. If I relent, he'll reach down my throat like a pelican feeding its young. Given the condition of his hands by 8 P.M., I may as well be getting my uvula massaged by a gloveless bridge troll. I have to protect myself and so should you. Here's a list of supplies I carry around the house in a giant backpack.

1. Two falcon gloves
2. One large bottle of hydrogen peroxide
3. A hockey mask
4. Aloe
5. One pair of burlap chaps (prevents scratching)
6. A 4 × 4 sheet of Plexiglas
7. Two units of type-O blood
8. One shower cap

9. A jar of peanut butter (He hates it. Works like garlic on a vampire.)

10. Racquetball glasses

11. Pelican repellant

12. A welder's helmet (for when hockey mask and shower cap have already been used)

13. Skin-grafting kit

14. Zithromax (any potent antibiotic will work here)

15. An air horn (think of this as a panic button)

16. A smoke machine

17. Echinacea

18. One crash-test dummy

19. Two packages of PowerGel (Sometimes the assault lasts for hours. Need fuel.)

20. One mouth guard

21. An extra shirt

22. One eyebrow pencil

23. Two kidneys (on ice—very important)

When all of that fails, just tickle them.

Of course, my kids are absolutely adorable. And so are yours. They are our first choice for people we would let excavate our throat, and there's no one we'd rather have puncture our lung. We always hurt the ones we love.

Oh, the Things You'll No Longer Need

Saying good-bye to your old, childless life means getting rid of things. You need to make room for plastic oboes and large colorful cloth cubes that roar, ribbit, and hiss. I've compiled a list of all the items in and around your home that will go completely unused for about a year after you have children.

1. Your bicycle

2. Novels

3. Vases

4. Skis

5. The alarm clock

6. Chopsticks

7. Your sexy voice

8. Fishing poles

9. Your friends' phone numbers

10. Decorative bowls

11. Negligee (did I spell that right?)

12. Tennis racquets

13. Magazine subscriptions

14. Sex toys

15. Jewelry

16. Scuba gear

17. Concert tickets

18. Indoor plants

19. Napkin rings

20. Napkins

21. Your cool leather jacket

22. Floor lamps

23. Anything made of glass

24. Exercise equipment (unless the cats like it)

25. Shoes with laces

26. Travel books

27. Yarn

28. Your tuba (Only for people who play the tuba. I don't play the tuba, so what do I know?)

Oh, the Things You'll No Longer Do

Be prepared to not do any of the following things for at least four years after having children. These are in no particular order.

1. Floss
2. Learn
3. Canoe
4. Say no to pizza
5. Sit down
6. Get a promotion
7. Dream
8. Illicit drugs
9. Pottery
10. Take more than eight minutes to eat a meal
11. Oral sex
12. Sex
13. Woodworking
14. Follow politics
15. Have a great pair of socks
16. Yoga
17. Set your alarm
18. Groom

19. Go antiquing

20. Stretch

21. Drink enough water

22. Hold in a fart

23. Fart with confidence

24. Hang glide

25. Make a salad

26. Get a colonoscopy

27. Listen to a complete story

28. Think slowly

29. See the dentist

30. Use a hot tub

31. Iron something

32. Karate

33. Emergency couples therapy

34. Get a new driver's license

35. Tailgate

36. Like your hair

37. Visit France

38. Crochet

39. Have stamps

40. Enter REM sleep

41. Know where your shoes are

42. Lose weight

Oh, but the New and Wonderful New Things You'll Get to Do

There are, indeed, countless things you will no longer be able to do after having children, like grooming, learning, stretching, and snorkeling. But don't fret. Here are just a few of the amazing new things you'll get to do instead.

1. Butter a piece of toast while peeing

2. Brush someone's teeth against his will

3. Blow on food while it's in someone else's mouth

4. Help someone else blow on food while it's in someone else's mouth

5. Eat food that has fallen out of someone else's mouth

6. Eat food you found on the floor

7. Eat food you found on the mantle

8. Eat candy you found in a shoe

9. Put someone in a Bob the Builder costume while fighting off diarrhea

10. Visit a psychiatrist

11. Wipe somebody's nose with your bare hand

12. Eat baby food

13. Blame a fart on a child

14. Get someone dressed while you're in the shower

15. Cut up a grape

16. Almost agree to cut up a raisin

17. Pretend to enjoy the flavor of a prune

18. Ask someone why their hair smells like yogurt

19. Ask someone why their hair smells like your antiperspirant

20. Put someone else's toenail clippings in your pocket

21. Let someone watch you pee as they stare blankly while eating a Popsicle

Reasons Your Toddler Might Be Freaking Out

It's hard to be a kid, especially when you consider all the possible things that might be upsetting them. These are all guesses. Children of this age are incapable of explaining why they've lost their minds.

1. His sock is on wrong.

2. His lip tastes salty.

3. His shirt has a tag on it.

4. The car seat is weird.

5. He's hungry, but can't remember the word "hungry."

6. Someone touched his knee.

7. He's not allowed in the oven.

8. I picked out the wrong pants.

9. His brother looked at him.

10. His brother didn't look at him.

11. His hair is heavy.

12. We don't understand what he said.

13. He doesn't want to get out of the car.

14. He wants to get out of the car by himself.

15. The iPad has a password.

16. His sleeve is touching his thumb.

17. He doesn't understand how Popsicles are made.

18. The inside of his nose stinks.

19. Chicken is gross.

20. A balloon he got six months ago is missing.

21. A puzzle piece won't fit in upside down.

22. I gave him the wrong blue crayon.

23. The gummy vitamin is too firm.

24. The Internet is slow.

25. He jumped off the sofa and we weren't watching.

26. He's not allowed to touch fire.

27. Everything is wrong with his coat.

28. There's a dog within a seventy-mile radius.

29. A shoe should fit either foot.

30. I asked him a question.

31. His brother is talking.

32. He can't lift a pumpkin.

33. He can't have my keys.

34. The cat is in his way.

35. The cat won't let him touch its eyeball.

36. The inside of his cheek feels rough.

37. Things take too long to cook.

38. He has too much food in his mouth.

39. He sneezed.

40. He doesn't know how to type.

41. The garbage disposal is going to eat him.

42. His mom is taking a shower.

43. Someone knocked over his tower.

44. He got powdered sugar on his pants.

45. The yogurt won't stay on his spoon.

46. EVERYTHING IS TOO HOT.

The Only Chart
Parents Will Ever Need

*I promise, it will seem as if your children are at their
most energetic when you're at your least. The graph below
proves just that: parental energy and a child's
needs are most frequently at odds with each other. I think
it's nature's way of encouraging kids to learn to play
by themselves.*

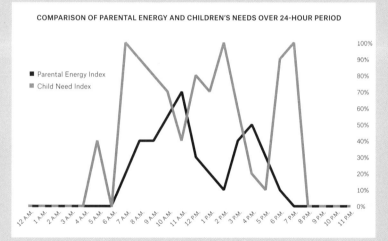

COMPARISON OF PARENTAL ENERGY AND CHILDREN'S NEEDS OVER 24-HOUR PERIOD

- Parental Energy Index
- Child Need Index

As you can see, nighttime is easy because both energy
and need are at zero. But notice the spike that occurs at
5 A.M. Generally there is some sort of waking during this
hour, which requires a bit of attention at a time when
parental energy has flatlined.

At 7 A.M., need is at one hundred. During this hour, the parent is awake, but has yet to imbibe any caffeine. This is a difficult sixty minutes.

By 8 A.M., need has dropped slightly, and now, having slugged back some coffee, the parent has plenty of energy. Meanwhile, the child may have wandered off to play by himself, only calling for his mother every five minutes or so to help him find something. Usually this time is spent doing dishes or answering emails.

By 11 A.M., the parent is feeling pretty good, but when lunch comes around energy starts to dip, and falls consistently for the next two hours. During this stretch, a three-year-old child is struggling with fatigue as well, but instead of napping, he insists on having a rave or riding the parent like a horse throughout the house. This energy peaks at 2 P.M. when the parent is trying desperately just to keep her eyes open. This is a good hour to invent a game that involves lying down. (See page 26 for more games to play while lying down.) "Put stuff on top of Mommy" is a good one. It's possible to lose consciousness, either because you've fallen asleep or suffocated under the weight of a giant stuffed bear.

This brief rest generally results in a resurgence of energy, but the child has gotten through his difficult hours and now wanders off to remove all the sheets from the bed, or build a tower with cans of cat food.

Now is a good time to make dinner. Once everyone is seated at the table, the children suddenly appear to have ingested some form of street speed. The parent, on the other hand, is exhausted and ready to go home to a nice tumbler of scotch, but realizes she already is home and weeps softly on the inside.

From 6 P.M. until bedtime is complete chaos. At 7:15 or so, a child might be seen chasing his parent through the house while wielding a flashlight and screaming something about batteries. From 7 P.M. to 8 P.M., the only real option is to have a glass of wine (a big one). This, of course, causes you to fall asleep at 9 P.M. and when that 5 A.M. waking occurs, the parent realizes that she only gets an hour off per day.

Games You Can Play
While Lying Down

For those times where your energy is at its lowest, I've invented some games that require virtually no effort. When done correctly, they'll allow you to catch a quick nap.

1. Put All the Sunglasses and Hats on Daddy

2. Take Off Daddy's Socks

3. Put Mommy's Socks on Daddy

4. Try to Lift Daddy

5. Put the Cats on Daddy

6. Wind Monster (Just blow on them. If you really commit, you might pass out and that's the same as sleeping.)

7. Human Body Tower (also known as The Sandwich)

8. Pull Daddy Around on a Sleeping Bag

9. Breath-Holding Competition

10. Daddy's a Giant Conga Drum (Think of it as acupressure therapy.)

11. Daddy's a Guitar! (Make sure kids' fingernails are clipped. Also, no picks.)

12. Put Daddy in "Sofa Jail"

13. Pretend We're Sleeping Cats! (May turn into real sleeping.)*

14. Decorate Daddy's Jeans with Sidewalk Chalk

15. Put Makeup on Daddy (Messier than #14, but still worth it.)

16. Turn Daddy into a Burrito (a.k.a. "The Mummy"; requires a beige flat sheet and patience)

17. Pretend to Eat Daddy (no utensils)

18. Vacuum Daddy **

19. Embalm Daddy ***

---

* CAUTION: This game ends abruptly when a child jumps on your face. I suggest wearing a hockey mask (see How to Defend Yourself Against a Toddler Attack, page 12).

** SUGGESTION: Vacuum should be in the "off" position. Also, keep your shirt on.

*** WARNING: Make *sure* child does not know what embalming is.

Tips for Traveling with Small Children

*I don't recommend it, but eventually you'll have to travel
on an airplane with your kids. Whatever the reason,
I have some advice. I'm sure there are lists in parenting
magazines that tell you to "Bring plenty of snacks,"
or "Don't forget a change of clothes." Even a mother
chimpanzee knows to do this stuff when she flies.
Here's some advice for human parents who have the
no-brainer things figured out already.*

1. Bring at least seven different sizes and kinds of headphones. You'll lose two, and four of them "DON'T FIT RIGHT!!!!"

2. You'll have to change a nasty diaper in the lavatory. Start stretching now (remember, you already gave up yoga).

3. Ninety minutes into the flight you will have suicidal thoughts. Do not panic; this is completely normal. You're not going to kill yourself, it just makes you feel better to think that it's an option.

4. Some people say, "Oh, just give them Benadryl and they'll sleep the whole flight." Well, if you want to gamble with your own sanity, go for it. About 30 percent of kids become hyper after taking anti-histamines. If that happens, jump out.

5. Watching *Die Hard with a Vengeance* just once isn't going to do any permanent damage to your three-year-old.

6. The answer to, "When are we going to be there?" is "If you keep asking me that, never." WARNING: If your children don't understand the concept of "never" (and they probably don't) this answer might result in an existential conversation about eternity and death. While that *can* burn through a nice chunk of the flight, it's not the time or the place.

7. Go ahead and be one of those weirdos who brings a pillow on the airplane with you. But, please, no pajama pants for the grown-ups.

8. Mix a good amount of Valium with coffee. You need to be alert, but relaxed. I would say five milligrams and a triple espresso, but I have a pretty high tolerance.

9. REMEMBER: When the flight is over, you still have about an hour of hell trying to stop your kids from climbing on the baggage carousel or running out the door and boarding an Avis courtesy bus.

10. Even if you're going to visit family, there's only so much they can do for you while you're there. Most of the time, everything is actually harder.

ENJOY YOUR TRAVELS.

Some Things I'll Miss

When you're in the parenting trenches it's difficult to have perspective. But sometimes, when a calm comes over the home and you find yourself smiling instead of angrily buttering toast, you realize, "Wow, I'm going to miss these things when he's older."

1. How much he wants me around

2. How he always skips the number four when counting to ten

3. That he thinks there are a million pennies in a dollar

4. The way he pronounces *S* from the back of his throat

5. How he takes his shirt off by sticking his arms through the neck hole

6. That he doesn't know when to end a hug

7. That we do three kinds of kisses, "gentle," "wet," and "dry." (If I could keep only one, it would be "gentle.")

8. That he can't say the alphabet without singing it

9. How uncomplicated he is

10. That he hides his shoes inside of mine

11. His inability to lie

12. The look on his face when he tries to lie

13. The year he said "I DO!" instead of "Yes"

14. How small he looks on the sofa

15. That he eats a hot dog like corn on the cob

16. His complete lack of self-consciousness

17. That he made up my new favorite word: "whobody."
    "Whobody can race to the kitchen first?!"

NO PERMANENT DAMAGE

Some of the most amazing and creative
people I've met have terrible parents.
So, when you forget to have your child
vaccinated and then find him chewing
on a rusty bolt he found in the shed—
a shed you didn't know he was in because
you were Tweeting—understand that
mistakes like these are the seeds from
which an artist grows.

The Wrong Kind of Games

I know it's rough to entertain kids, especially on weekends in the winter. It's tempting to let things go a little nuts, but don't think too far outside the box and end up getting someone injured or causing an uncleanable mess. (Of course, any permanent damage caused here will only result in a great short-story topic for their college fiction-writing class.)

1. Find the Raccoon
2. Boat Races in the Toilet
3. Brush the Cat's Teeth
4. Try Out the Toothbrush You Found Behind the Radiator
5. Shave Daddy (This may seem like a Game You Can Play While Lying Down, page 26, but it's simply too dangerous. Sorry.)
6. Hide Mommy's Passport
7. Dental Hygienist
8. Pet the Squirrel
9. Satellite Dish Repair Man
10. Crawl Space Hide-and-Seek

11. Free Rein with the Garden Hose (Use Any Setting!)

12. Fun with Grout

13. Kids Clean the Litter Box!

14. Circle Mommy's Problem Areas

15. Will it Flush?

16. Painting with Refried Beans

17. Couch-Jumping with Cake

18. Is This Socket Grounded?

19. Prune the Magnolia

20. Search for Roadkill

21. Eat the Parachute

22. Bee Beards!

23. Mosh Pit in Mommy's Room

24. Decorative Bowl Toss

25. Is This Edible?

26. Chimney Sweep

27. Mr. Fork Fingers

Never play Mr. Fork Fingers.

Signs You're Going Native

In anthropological research, the term "going native" is used to describe a situation in which a researcher comes to identify so much with her subjects that she gives up her "real" life to live among the people she's been studying. Here are some warning signs that you might be losing yourself in the culture of your kids.

1. Start wearing colorful pants

2. Say "super dupes" to an adult

3. Drink a juice box in public

4. Drink from a sippy cup

5. Become inappropriately excited upon spotting a train

6. Realize your playlist is more than 60 percent kids' music

7. Hum the *Strawberry Shortcake* theme song in the car—when you're alone

8. Decide it's "cute" to wear your hair in pigtails

9. Go down the stairs on your butt

10. Climb the stairs like a panther

11. Attempt to bribe co-workers with fruit snacks

12. Buy Velcro shoes for yourself because "they're super-convenient!"

13. Ask a waiter to direct you to "the potty"

14. Refer to yourself as "Daddy" when speaking to an adult

15. Have cheesy toast for dinner

16. Refuse to eat the skin on fruit

17. Refer to something as "yucky" or "icky"

18. Suddenly decide you no longer like oranges

Don't Trust
Your Instincts

Children are human, but that doesn't mean they're rational. Natural selection no longer drives their decision-making, so if you assume they have any sense of self-preservation, please know that you do so at your own peril (and theirs).

INSTINCT: **Come on, a child *must* understand what "hurry up" means, right?**

REALITY: Incorrect. To a kid, this request means, "Quick! Hide your shoes."

INSTINCT: **If left to his own devices, a child will stop eating cookies before he breaks into a cold sweat, slaps his brother, and starts weeping.**

REALITY: Nope.

INSTINCT: **Eventually a kid will become tired of TV and choose to stop watching it himself.**

REALITY: Somewhere there's an eighty-year-old man who's been watching *Pinky Dinky Doo* for seventy-seven years straight.

INSTINCT: Children innately understand that driving a car is something that requires concentration and focus.

REALITY: I'm sorry, but no. They think the car drives itself and you're just the lucky one who gets the seat with the big wheel. Therefore, this thing called "driving" is not a valid excuse for your inability to make them a sandwich.

INSTINCT: Kids will eat when they're hungry.

REALITY: No they won't. At least, I don't think so. I've never waited more than a few hours before promising them candy if they eat a kernel of corn.

INSTINCT: A toddler knows that jumping on his father's face might result in injury.

REALITY: Well, he might, but he doesn't care because it's hilarious.

Have fun out there!

No Need to Feel Guilty

*No matter how much food you leave for them, it's still
unacceptable to lock your kids in a room and go on a
cruise—that's bad parenting. But you can't be perfect all
the time. You should be allowed to nap once a year, right?
And don't feel guilty about doing any of these things
either (acceptable age range of child is three to seven).*

1. Pretending you're asleep

2. Lying about what day it is

3. Pretending you're deaf

4. Hiding a toy and telling your kid someone stole it

5. Breaking a toy on purpose and blaming your spouse

6. Giving your kid the hot dog that fell on the floor

7. Giving your kid the hot dog that fell in the sand

8. Telling your kid you'll "be right back," then staying away until they fall asleep

9. Faking a shoulder injury so you don't have to carry anyone

10. Saying, "Trevor is on vacation with his family."
(He's not, but you don't like Trevor or his mom.)

The Wrong Kind of Funny

I have a sarcastic sense of humor. Tragically, it's lost on my kids. So, because I'm your parenting spirit animal, I've put together five examples of how not to use hyperbole and sarcasm when speaking with children.

1. Do Not Exaggerate the Passage of Time for Comedic Effect

Twelve minutes into a fifteen-minute car ride, my five-year-old asked (for the eighth time) how much longer it was going to take to get to the zoo. When I responded, "A million years," he said, "Wait, for real life? A million years?" "No, buddy, not for real life. We'll be there in three minutes." "But that's *such a long time!*" he whined. And that's what I was trying to communicate: Any amount of time less than "we're here" would seem like forever. Does he understand why that's kind of funny? Of course not. Now he has no idea what a million is, and, well, neither do I, really.

2. Do Not Use Injury Hyperbole

The kids were attacking me in a loving way, and I said, "Don't jump on me like that or you'll rupture my spleen." You'll realize, throughout the course of explaining to your kid what a spleen is and why it's important, that you have no idea what a spleen is or why it's important.

3. Do Not Use Surrealist Sarcasm

I recently said to my three-year-old, "The day you actually brush your teeth without me asking, penguins will probably fly out of your butt." You'd think that might be funny to a kid until you realize they don't know for sure that penguins can't fly out of their butt. Don't say this unless you want your child to start insisting on wearing diapers again to avoid the room becoming engulfed in penguins when he brushes his teeth.

4. Do Not Exaggerate Your Anger

After a small argument about how much television Arlo (age three) was watching, I found myself explaining to him why I said I was going to "throw the iPad out the window and let the snowman eat it." Of course, I would never actually throw the iPad out the window (unless I wanted to explain to my wife why we needed a new one *with a retina screen*). My son's wide moose-brown eyes spoke to me. They said, "Daddy, why do you have to make up such horrible, horrible things?" I responded with, "I'm sorry. I was just kidding around. I won't throw the iPad out the window, and even if I did—which I wouldn't—the snowman doesn't have . . . never mind. You want to watch another *Super Why*?"

5. Do Not Exaggerate Using
Astronomical Distances

While on the swing, Arlo insisted, "Push me higher! Push me higher. Higher, Daddy! Higher!" It was relentless, so I made a joke that only adults would understand (and probably not laugh at because it's lame). "If I swing you any higher, you might go all the way around the bar and fly off and hit the moon." Cute, right? No. He wanted to get off immediately and go back inside, because if there's one thing he knows about astronomy, it's that the moon is really far away from the iPad.

How to Piss Off
Your Pediatrician

1. Say, "Well, I read on the Internet that . . . "

2. Tell him (or her) that you're thinking of following a "non-traditional vaccination schedule"

3. Ask more than three questions about the same topic

4. Ask him a personal question

5. Act like you know what you're talking about

6. Sit in his chair

7. Cry

8. Ask repeatedly, "This is hoof-and-mouth disease, isn't it?"

9. Bring your other children with you to the appointment

10. Ask her about your own medical situation. "You know, speaking of rashes, I have one on my shoulder. Can you take a look? No? Okay, cool."

11. Make an origami swan out of that ridiculous deli paper on the examination table

12. Ask, "What would you do if it was your kid?"

13. Act disinterested when he tries to tell you the story about that time he met Jackie Mason (maybe that's just our pediatrician)

14. Eat a tuna fish sandwich in his office (this goes for all doctors, and anyone else, I guess)

Go Ahead and Camp

It's easy to get too excited about the arrival of summer.
Here are some things you should keep in mind before
scheduling that family trip.

1. Starting a fire on purpose is really hard. Starting one on accident is very easy. It's kind of like making a baby.

2. All the kids' socks are wet within the first five minutes.

3. Your morning bathroom ritual will go from being your favorite part of the day to an hour of panic.

4. Your kids will each find a special rock, and one will promptly lose it. The entire weekend will be spent searching for the special rock.

5. You ever try to get a three-year-old to sit down? Now try it in a canoe.

6. Your child will develop a sudden fear of peeing outside (something he does all too frequently at home). Have fun taking him to the john in bare feet every hour.

7. You'll spend approximately 75 percent of your day explaining "what that noise was."

8. You'll talk incessantly about buying an RV. You'll never do it.

9. The guy at the campsite next to you might have a Confederate flag and call everyone "fella."

10. Even expensive freezer bags can't keep graham crackers dry.

11. Hiking involves a lot more arguing and carrying of children than you remembered.

12. Seeing a moose is not magical. It's terrifying.

13. You'll say, "I think that's poison oak" at least forty times and be right twice.

14. No matter your sleep position, there will be an acorn under your hip.

15. Tent farts.

And it's all totally worth it. Seriously, even the "cave rash" you'll all contract.

Reasons to
Avoid the Beach

I've given the beach plenty of chances. After five minutes, I'm sweaty, salty, and sting-y. That's not even remotely tolerable when you're alone, but when you also have two genetically unsuited children in tow it can result in side-by-side father/son tantrums.

1. Within thirty seconds of sitting down, both kids' suits are filled with sand.

2. Three-year-old Arlo throws a fit because he can't surf.

3. Silas trips and lands on a dead fish.

4. Arlo becomes obsessed with smelling Silas's hair and screaming, "YUCK POOP FISH!"

5. The strap on Mommy's top breaks, and a "creepy guy" sees her boob.

6. Since Daddy's not an Eagle Scout, he can't get the sun umbrella to stay up.

7. A gust of wind sends the sun umbrella flying down the beach. It lands on an attractive couple making out.

8. Arlo throws sand in Silas's face = Day over.

9. Both kids fall asleep in the car on the way home and will now be awake until 10 P.M.

10. Everyone wants to go back to the beach next weekend because even suffering is kind of fun when we do it together.

The Five Perils of International Travel

Many people take their small children abroad with great success. I know this because they tell me—frequently. They are brave souls. I prefer to stay local for now. I need the comforts of home, plus I'm pretty sure that the ancient caves of Cappadocia would be lost on a five-year-old. My children are filled with wonder when we visit a new grocery store, so I'll wait until they're unimpressed by that before making reservations for four to New Zealand. Why do I feel like that? I'll tell you.

1. Your kids won't adjust to a time change until the day you fly home. Have fun getting up at 3 A.M. or being five hours late for everything for a week and a half. On the airplane, your kid will be bonkers, lifting and lowering the tray table incessantly and jumping up and down on his chair until the final five minutes of the flight, when he will fall asleep.

2. Wifi on flights is too slow for Netflix. So if you didn't already download forty-seven episodes of his favorite show the night before, start taking advantage of the drink cart. Actually, scratch that. There's nothing worse than being on vacation with kids while hungover.

3. You didn't realize that kids need passports. Have a great trip home. Was the airport nice at least?

4. The milk is "weird" abroad. In Europe it's unrefrigerated and packaged in a box. In parts of Asia they don't even have milk. If you can get your kids to drink out of a coconut more than once, you're a magician.

5. In some countries, your only TV options are local channels and CNN International. I hope your young ones enjoy watching the revolution in Mongolia or fifty-year-old Italian men laughing at boobs.

On Being a Role Model

"Do as I say, not as I do." It's a phrase people have been saying since Al Gore invented children. And for good reason: we all want our kids to be better than us, but we're also old and set in our ways—either unable or unwilling to change ourselves and become better role models. Have you done any of these things?

1. Said, "Too much candy is bad for you" while opening a cupboard door to hide your face as you stuff it with M&Ms. (For more on this, see Safe Places to Eat Cookies, page 105.)

2. Yelled, "No yelling!"

3. Explained the importance of getting enough rest and then the next day explained that you're tired because you stayed up until 3 A.M. trying to find something to watch on Netflix.

4. Told him you're too tired to play tag, but then jumped out of your chair the moment you remembered there was ice cream in the freezer.

5. Without looking up from your phone, told your kid he's "logged too much screen time today."

6. Said, "Don't talk like that, you'll probably get in a sh*tload of trouble at school. I mean crapload . . . Just don't say bad words, okay?"

7. Told him, "It's important to respect the earth because it's our home!" as you threw away half a carton of milk because you can't fit it in the refrigerator.

8. Expressed how important it is to respect people's things while kicking one of his toys out of the way so you could get to the coffeemaker.

9. From your position lying down on an adjacent sofa, told him to sit up straight.

10. In the midst of biting your fingernails, told your kid to relax and be present.

I guess we never learn, do we?

Eight Dangers of
Green Parenting

*Let's be clear. By "green parenting," I mean being high on
pot. I may take some heat for this, but I can't see anything
good coming from it. Too many things can go wrong when
you smoke LEGAL marijuana while parenting. I'm not
just talking about the obvious stuff like accidentally setting
yourself on fire or baking a prune cake. Actually,
I am talking about those things. Here are some more.
If you're high right now you might not "get" this.
And look, I know that LEGAL marijuana can be used very
responsibly by people caring for children. Seriously.
But things can go wrong.*

1. Your phone might ring.

2. You could become confused and buy your kid a jean jacket.

3. A Lego piece will go missing. You'll look for an hour, only to find it in your pants. But it'll be a different Lego than the one that's missing. In fact, you don't even have this kind of Lego in your house. You become even more confused and buy your kid jean shorts.

4. You might get so hooked on an episode of *Dora* that you don't notice your kid left the house.

5. You *will* eat all the graham crackers and drink all the strawberry milk.

6. Your son might ask for a sandwich and you can't quite remember exaaaaactly what that is.

7. Your child might catch you petting the fern.

8. Your kid will say, "Daddy, you're not a rabbit, you just put oven mitts on your head."

What My Kid Dreams About

These are guesses, of course.

1. He makes friends with a hilarious chicken.

2. He's stuffing his diaper with a dozen phones.

3. He's on a raft with a beaver, a platypus, and a miniature elephant. They're in a bathtub full of melted cheese. In the distance he hears the faint sound of morning birds. It's 5 A.M. Time to wake up Mommy.

4. He's in a play but doesn't know his lines. (Even kids have this dream, right?)

5. He's driving a car while screaming, "I'm totally driving this car!"

6. He's riding a unicorn and screaming, "What's happening? This weird horse has a horn! I'm totally riding a horse with a horn!"

7. He goes out into the backyard where he sees someone on his favorite swing. He knows it's his brother but it looks like his grandfather. He yells "Boo Boo," but his grandfather says, "No, I'm Silas. Your brother." Then the grass turns into a mouth and swallows him. Time to wake up Daddy.

8. He's forced to listen to a continuous loop of his mother saying, "I'll be right back." Time to wake up Mommy.

9. His teeth are falling out. (Usually indicates his fear of losing his "special" quarter.)

UNDERSTANDING YOUR CO-PARENT

All you really need to know is this: When your co-parent says, "Come help me," what she or he really means is, "Please join me in suffering through this situation neither of us can control."

You Deserve a Break

No matter how much we love our children, we're also desperate to get away from them. Before having a family, taking out the garbage was a chore. Now it's a thirty-second vacation. Other things that used to be a hassle but are now considered sweet gifts:

1. Power-washing the house

2. Picking up someone at the airport

3. Going to the dentist

4. Taking things to the dump

5. Donating stuff to the Salvation Army

6. Cleaning the gutters

7. Helping a neighbor power-wash his house

8. Unclogging the toilet

9. Giving blood

10. Searching for whatever it is in the house that smells bad

11. Canvassing the neighborhood

12. Vacuuming the car

13. Chaperoning a rave

14. Getting a wart removed

15. Going to physical therapy

16. Untangling cords

17. Filling out insurance forms

18. Jump-starting a stranger's car

19. Printing something

20. Cleaning out a sump pump

21. Doing anything that involves driving

22. Taking the cat to the vet

23. Serving on a sequestered jury

24. Disposing of hazardous waste

25. Crop dusting

26. Manning the neighborhood polling place

27. Minor surgery

28. Getting car-jacked

29. Participating in a drug trial

30. Going to rehab

One Hour Inside My Wife's Brain

The good news is: You aren't doing this parenting thing alone, right? RIGHT? If you're a single parent, JESUS HAROLD CHRIST. HOW ARE YOU DOING THAT? Send me your address and I'll mail you forty hugs and a couple of bucks (money, not male deer). But co-parenting has its own difficulties. It's important that I understand my wife. I spent some time writing down what I believed she was thinking about over the course of around three hours. I think this might only help the dads, though, but I'm no gender expert.

1. My phone just made a noise. I'll get Jason out of the shower to ask him what it is.

2. I wonder if Silas will have a good singing voice.

3. I want to be outside ALL THE TIME.

4. Actually, forget that, I hate bugs.

5. I think Jason needs a pair of light-colored jeans. His black jeans only look good with colored shirts.

6. I want some cheese.

7. I bet my hair is really flat right now. I should fluff it up.

8. Oh, I'm gonna massage my own shoulder.

9. My kids understand me. All I need is my kids!

10. I can't believe I drank caffeine. I'm so tweaked.

11. Jason drinks so much coffee. Is this how he feels all the time? No wonder he's moody!

12. I think Jason should stop drinking caffeine.

13. I wonder if I'll ever read a book again.

14. I want to move to L.A. or maybe the Virgin Islands, actually maybe Montana or Wyoming.

15. No, here's good. I like it here. Really.

16. I wonder if Jason loves our cats as much as I do.

17. Where are my glasses?

18. Jason has never once known where my glasses are so I'll ask him if he knows.

19. Someone broke in and stole my glasses.

20. Oh, here they are.

21. I think it would be okay for a married couple to stay married and committed but just live in different houses.

22. I bet Jason *could* get a tan. I mean, his arms are kinda tan so . . .

23. I wonder what kind of cheese we have.

24. I really like Jason's eggplant-colored T-shirt. I should remind him that he looks good in that. I'll text him now because otherwise I'll forget.

25. I don't believe in vitamins.

26. I could eat all my meals from the samples at Whole Foods.

27. Someone stole my keys. Never mind, here they are.

28. I think I'll be on the PTA when Silas goes to school. I'm smart and have good opinions.

29. When does Trader Joe's open in the morning? I want some more of those mini quiches.

30. Silas woke up crying at 10 P.M. I have to call Jason because he's in the city and there's nothing he can do about it, but I still want him to know it happened.

31. I think I could have been the Bachelorette.

32. Jason has a better sense of smell than I do, but I don't think he hears things very well.

33. Note to self: Express concern to Jason about the volume of his headphones.

34. He's driving back from the city so I'll call him and tell him. No, actually I'll text him. I hope he doesn't text while driving. I wonder how fast he's driving.

What Parents Say
Instead of F✲ck

After feeding, comforting, dressing, teaching, entertaining,
and loving our children, the remaining 37 percent
of parenting is trying not to say the F-word in front of
them. But having been subjected to five straight years
of sleep deprivation, my wife needs to let things fly
sometimes. Being a good mom, she's unwittingly created
her own G-rated language of anger, frustration, and
pain. Here are some of my favorites.

"MOTHER FRUIT!" "Mother fruit" comes in three colorful variations:

"Fruit on a fruit stick"

"Holy mother of fruit"

"Mother of fruit on a fruit stick," and then, if she's really mad . . .

"HOLY MOTHER OF FRUIT ON A FRUITIN' FRUIT STICK"

Questions: What is a fruit stick? I've heard of fruit skin, fruit strip, and even fruit stripe (like the gum), but fruit stick sounds like part of a package air-dropped by the Red Cross. What is "mother of fruit"? I believe that would simply be a tree, but yelling "TREE" doesn't really provide much satisfaction. Here are some other kid-friendly swears I've heard in and around the parent-sphere.

1. Son of a biscuit eater (the origin of this is obvious, but it makes absolutely no sense)

2. Sweet honey iced tea (predominantly used in the South)

3. Holy shiitake (clever way of tacking something on the end to make it G-rated)

4. Fudge crackers (this sounds like something Goofy would say when he's mad)

5. Fudge muffin (I find this to be quite disgusting)

6. Fraggle Rock (unfortunately, this parent has "gone native")

7. Bunnyfluffer (I vote no on this one)

8. Donkey crevice (I want to like this, but "crevice" kind of ruins it for me)

9. Sockcutter (again, I understand the origin, but this is nonsense)

10. Manischewitz (used mostly on the Upper West Side of Manhattan and in Israel)

11. Philadelphia cream cheese (nice product placement!)

12. Fudgington valley (huh?)

13. Fire truck (another parent lost to the natives)
14. Melon farmer (this is desperate)
15. Fluffernutting Ice Capades (this parent might be having a stroke)
16. Mother of pearl (has a certain old-timey appeal)
17. Smurfin (no)
18. Farknarkles (we have a winner)
19. Fart nugget (I've used this one myself, but as a term of endearment)
20. Fudge puppets (too much fudge? I agree)
21. Hamburger patty (I like the inclusion of "patty" here)
22. Son of a birch bark canoe (I wonder if this parent has tried lithium)
23. Fuzz buckets (really rolls off the tongue and has just the right degree of absurdity, A+)
24. What the ham? (this person is hungry)

Of course, sometimes we fail, or simply really need to let a real one fly. It's totally okay, just remember to give yourself a time-out afterward.

Home Schoolin'

*There's probably no better way to ruin a marriage
than embarking on a joint teaching venture.
Most parents can't agree on how often children should
bathe, which makes me hesitant to even imagine
what would happen when it's time to teach the kids
about the JFK assassination. So unless one of you
is already a teacher, or you're in a traveling circus of
some kind and have no other option, I suggest you
avoid it. Here's why we decided against it.*

1. I recently had to Google "parallelogram."

2. It took five tries for Google to even recognize that I was trying to spell parallelogram.

3. My wife thinks a trapezoid is a kind of triangle. (Is it?)

4. I get lost in the mall.

5. My wife believes in astrology but doesn't know why fire is hot.

6. I've never successfully made a cursive upper-case *D* or *S*.

7. Recently, my wife said, "So Silas, to count all the way to one hundred, you go ten, twenty, thirty, forty, fifty, sixty, seventy, eighty, ninety, and then a bunch of the other numbers in between."

8. I got a 900 on my SAT.

9. My wife thinks P.T. Barnum and John Wilkes Booth are the same person.

10. I don't know how; to use semicolons.

11. Neither of us knows why pee is yellow.

12. Neither of us has read a book in at least six years.

13. We don't know where salt water comes from.

14. My wife recently asked, "Egypt is in . . . Africa?" A teacher needs to know that for sure.

15. Porpoise or dolphin? No idea.

How to Know If Your Wife Has Been Drinking

We all need to cut loose every now and then. But you probably don't drink quite as much now as you did before kids (if you drink more, that's cool, too), so your tolerance is way down. Be careful out there. Here are some danger signs. Knowing them can prevent a situation where your wife (or husband) decides she (yes, or he) wants to move to Peru for no good reason.

1. She stares up at the moon and yells something like, "I don't sleep at all at night and that makes me a little bitchy during the days, so if you don't like it you can just stick it up your butt!"

2. She's crying, but she's not sad.

3. She wants to have sex, but you're scared of her.

4. She wants to call her best friend from high school.

5. She starts talking about her favorite cartoon from childhood.

6. She specifically says, "You're not even paying any goddamn attention to me, are you?" Before you can answer, she's calling her best friend from high school.

7. She hasn't talked about the kids for thirty seconds.

8. When you mention the kids, she responds, "Who? Oh, right. THEM!"

9. She says, and I quote, "Sometimes I have dreams that I own a tiger but it's gentle like a house cat."

10. She tries to make crêpes.

Nap Guilt

*Parents aren't allowed to nap, so when it happens,
it's emotionally loaded. I once fell asleep in bed for two
hours while my wife entertained both children
(one of them had screaming gas pains). Here are my
thoughts in chronological order upon waking.*

1. Oh God, that was amazi . . . wait.

2. Oh no, it's been two hours.

3. There must be a catch. This can't be real.

4. I'm too afraid to get up.

5. She has never taken a nap.

6. I don't hear anything downstairs. Did she take the
    kids to France because I fell asleep during the day?

7. Okay, relax, you're just gonna have to pay this back
    somehow.

8. Oh, it's Sunday too. Sundays are supposed to be
    special.

9. Oh no, someone's coming up the stairs.

10. Do I pretend I'm still asleep or do I get up real quick?

11. I'll just say I'm sick.

12. No! You know what? I deserved that nap!

13. No I didn't.

Napping Isn't the Only Way to Torture Your Co-parent

Your partner is the person with whom you share life's most heinous but rewarding chore. Your co-parent needs to know that you're looking out for her or him. Here are some ways to fail at that. Many of these have repercussions for both of you.

1. Get a cold

2. Get a haircut

3. Visit an old friend

4. Eat the kids' food (this is grounds for divorce)

5. Engage in "Netflix infidelity" whereby you watch future episodes of a television program you had previously agreed to watch together

6. Take up a hobby

7. Get drunk

8. Quit drinking

9. Take a shower

10. Let a three-year-old take a nap after 3:30 P.M.

11. Go to bed before the kids

12. Tell the kids they're not allowed to watch any more TV right before you leave for work

13. Sustain any kind of injury

14. Give a kid chocolate after 7 P.M. when it's not "your night"

15. Buy a child RAD shoes . . . with laces

16. Teach a child to whistle

17. Teach a child how to create a Pandora station

18. Teach a child how to control the volume on the television

19. Mention something to the kids about possibly, maybe, just maybe going for ice cream seven hours before it's okay to go for ice cream

How to Maintain
the Magic

*It's far too easy to forget about your relationship when
you're so busy tending to the needs of young kids.
But, you know what they say: happy parents, happy kids.
My point is, if your marriage is being neglected (I hate
that word—marriage isn't a puppy), you'll break up
and then have to do all this stuff by yourself and no one
wants that. So, be sure to maintain the magic in your
soul-union by following my advice.*

1. Schedule sex, but be realistic. Try just once a week (Thursdays work well). And stick to it *no matter what!* Unless, of course, you're too tired.

2. Go out to dinner at 5 P.M. so the baby sitter doesn't have to "do bedtime." It's super-fun because you'll be the only two there who aren't over seventy.

3. Sleep in separate beds. Weird, right? But look, parents aren't having sex at night (or in the morning) anyway. This way, when SPECIAL THURSDAY rolls around, it'll feel like you're "doing it" in a hotel (to one of you at least) and that's sexy, right? I have no idea.

4. Read to each other. I'm kidding.

5. I can't stress this enough: Couples stay together primarily because they like the same television shows.

6. For the dudes: Buy flowers. I know, I know. Listen, I have no idea why this works so consistently and so flawlessly, but it does. Don't spend too much time thinking about it. Just do it.

7. Dudettes: Don't forget Special Thursdays, unless we do too. Also, buy us socks; it makes us feel like we're being taken care of. No, I can't explain why that is. Oh, and when we're in the bathroom, don't ask, "Are you almost done?"

Ridiculous Apologies

One of the most important things to remember when you're a co-parent is that everything is your fault. Just suck it up and apologize. I'm sorry...

1. I squeezed your foot incorrectly while massaging it.

2. I said "sh*t" in front of our son and his teacher, and his teacher's mother.

3. I replied with, "How the hell would I possibly know that?" when you asked me why a YouTube video wouldn't load.

4. I chewed a tortilla chip too loudly.

5. I make fun of the goat cheese you eat every night that smells like the foot of a medieval peasant.

6. I bent the stem on one of your earrings while using it to pop the SIM card out of your phone.

7. The universal remote doesn't seem to be functioning in an intuitive manner.

8. The patio rug I bought doesn't match the magnolia bush like you thought it would.

9. I don't put my used Q-tips in the nice ceramic tray you were kind enough to place on my desk with a "Put your gross Q-tips here J" note attached to it.

The Duties of a Twenty-First-Century Father

Some things about fatherhood never change. A father is still in charge of killing dinner and defending his family from rogue bandits. Fine, we're responsible for slightly less masculine stuff, such as:

1. Rebooting things

2. Syncing things

3. Lifting things

4. Hiring other people to lift things

5. Cooling off food with our GIANT MAN LUNGS

6. Mowing (I've never seen a woman mowing the lawn. The mere thought is comical and I'm not sure why.)

7. KILLING THINGS (bugs)

8. Plunging (toilets)

9. Carrying (children, groceries . . . that's pretty much it)

10. Fixing things (electronics only)

11. Hiring people to fix everything else

12. Talking to the people hired to fix everything else

13. Pumping (gas)

14. Grilling (like mowing, I've never seen a woman use an outdoor grill)

15. Answering the phone when the call is from an unlisted number

16. Carving (roasts, initials, etc.)

17. Investigating strange noises after 8 P.M.

18. Calling the police (because you're too afraid to investigate a nighttime sound)

Fourteen at Forty

If you're a young parent, nice job; you did it the right way. You had kids before you were too tired to fully appreciate them. My wife and I didn't have our first until we were thirty-six and thirty-five. Now that we're both over forty and our kids are at their most energetic, we often wish we'd . . .

Hang on, my wife would like to say something:

"IT'S ALL JASON'S FAULT BECAUSE HE WAITED

FIVE YEARS TO PROPOSE TO ME.

WE COULD HAVE DONE

ALL OF THIS MUCH EARLI . . ."

Okay, she's gone. Sorry about that.

Here are fourteen things I know about myself at forty years old that I didn't know when I was thirty. I hope this can be of some help to those of you still trying to find your way through the forest of enlightenment (no idea what that means).

1. I can *occasionally* wear sandals and not feel like a guy who wears sandals.

2. I'm finished experimenting with facial hair.

3. A hug from one of my sons is the only thing that stops time.

4. I'm not Zen enough to understand the rules for being Zen.

5. Real men sit down to pee if they're super tie-tie.

6. Whatever age I am when I die, there *will* be a zit somewhere on my body.

7. My wife loves me deeply, but she also might want to kill me.

8. I'm only good for about five more rounds of trying to enjoy tea.

9. It's not that I'm indecisive; there are just way too many fonts.

10. Being happy is a pointless goal. It's simply a side effect of doing something I enjoy.

11. It's okay to avoid someone completely just because of their name.

12. I'll never wear slacks.

13. Whiskey tastes bad for a good reason.

14. This list will be ridiculous in ten years when my gray handlebar mustache is stained brown from tea and I'm ironing slacks.

Without Mom, There Is No Us

I am in a perpetual state of awe about how my amazing wife is able to maintain her grace throughout all the insanity. Maybe it's a hormone that's released in women, or maybe she's just particularly amazing. Either way, I'm blown away by . . .

1. Her patience

2. Her confidence

3. Her persistence

4. The intimidating speed at which she can make a sandwich

5. How she always knows the right thing to say when one of our kids is sad

6. How quickly she can snap out of a bad mood

7. That she doesn't get angry when I find her secret stash of candy and eat the whole bag

8. That she's able to hold her tongue while I incorrectly assemble a piece of IKEA furniture

9. Her sense of humor

10. Her sense of humor about herself

11. How much she's given up, and how much she appreciates what she's gained in return

12. That she believed I could be a writer

13. That the funniest parts of this book were probably her idea

14. That this list made her cry (crossing my fingers . . . and yes, it did)

LOWERING YOUR STANDARDS

Let your home be exactly what it is:
a scared-straight program for prospective
parents. Open your doors to those special
couples thinking of having children
of their own. They need to know what
they're getting into and that, despite their
best intentions, their child, like yours,
will often be naked on the floor eating
yogurt with his hands.

Baby Wipes Forever

*I'm not proud of it, but on my list of priorities,
"conserving paper" is right above "inventing a car that
runs on pee." If you told me I had to stop using a box a day
of unscented baby wipes, I would say, "Well, then,
I guess this is the end, isn't it?" When I change a diaper,
I lay out a dozen wipes like I'm setting up a game
of wipe solitaire. We have a box in every room and use
them for a variety of off-label uses, including:*

1. Degreasing my phone

2. Crushing bugs

3. Moistening a temporary tattoo

4. Wiping down the refrigerator handles

5. Creating a moist mummy hand for picking up a yogurt-soaked cracker

6. Giving myself a crotch bath

7. Cleaning mulch off a hot dog

8. Wiping snot off the window

9. Wiping snot off the iPad

10. Spot-cleaning my jeans

11. Removing the cheese from a grilled cheese sandwich

12. Removing the peanut butter from a peanut butter and jelly sandwich

13. Removing cheese and peanut butter from my sock

14. Cleaning puke off a shoe

15. Prying a raisin off the bottom of a shoe

16. Cleaning a shoe print off of someone's face

When Listening
Is Impossible

Kids talk constantly, and usually do so with complete disregard to whether we can hear them. Because I care about all of you, here's a list of a few things that you can yell from another room when you can't tell what your kid said because you were busy giving CPR to a pet. They might find your response confusing, as it will often be a non sequitur. But at least this should buy you some time to finish paying your taxes, or have sex (j/k. No one does that).

1. Oh, that? I think it's broken or maybe Mommy lost it.

2. I heard about that!

3. SUPER DUPES, ZONKSTERS, ZONK-CITY, COOL BEANS KIDDO! (You get the idea.)

4. Are you touching the table with your foot again? Awesome.

5. Okay! Let me take my pills first.

6. No, it's not too hot. Just eat it.

7. No hitting or slamming anything.

8. We don't have the right kind of batteries.

9. Uh oh. That doesn't sound good.

10. I'm on the toilet! (Obviously, there's no need to actually be on the toilet. It won't matter to them anyway.)

11. Call 911.

12. Okay, just take your shoes off.

13. Of course! Just put your shoes on first.

14. Cool! Just don't eat it.

15. Well, if it smells like food, it's probably food.

16. Can't right now. On. Fire.

17. Okay, just wash your hands.

18. One sec, I'm almost done vomiting.

19. Ask your mother.

I hope you can make good use of these. Oh, and good news for the women: Most of these will also work on your husband.

WAKE UP! It's Morning

If you enjoy watching people struggle, I welcome you to my home on a particularly hectic weekday.

INT. SMALL BEDROOM (1), MORNING: Jason, a father in his early forties, sleeps alone in a bed on the floor in an unadorned room.

MASTER BEDROOM: Lindsay, the mother, sleeps in a king-size bed. Beside her is a small sleeping child. This is Arlo. His foot rests on the mother's cheek.

SMALL BEDROOM (2): Silas, a cute five-year-old boy, opens and closes his dresser drawers in a manner suggesting that he's trying to make as much noise as possible.

SILAS (yelling): Daddy! Where's my blue shirt with the octopus things on it?!??!!

BACK TO SMALL BEDROOM (1): Jason stirs, muttering something to himself. His eyes open slowly.

JASON: It's dirty, wear something else.

SILAS (from small bedroom (2)): But I want it!

SMALL BEDROOM (1): Jason rolls out of bed, reaches for his phone to check the time, and exhales, exasperated.

CUT TO MASTER BEDROOM: Lindsay is still sleeping despite Arlo jumping up and down on the bed.

ARLO: MOMMY MOMMY MOMMY

CUT TO KITCHEN, MOMENTS LATER: The Good family has risen and it is time to prepare breakfast at Downton. Silas sits at the kitchen table. Father, hair a mess and wearing jeans but no shirt, leans against the counter, chugging coffee. From upstairs, we hear Arlo.

ARLO: NO! I DON WANNA TAKE OFF DYPUR!

SILAS: Daddy, I want an egg with the soft kind of yellow part.

ARLO (from upstairs): GWEEN SOCKS!

LINDSAY (from upstairs): Jace, have you seen Arlo's green socks?

JASON (yelling): NO!

SILAS (watching a pair of rainbow socks and a rolled-up diaper tumble down the stairs): Daddy, I said I wanted an egg.

ARLO (still in pajamas on Lindsay's hip): GWEEN SOCKS!

LINDSAY: Arlo, I don't know where your green socks are!

SILAS: Egg!

LINDSAY: Oh, for Christ's sake. Fine. Jace, can you make Silas's snack? Make sure you put in some protein and don't use that huge ice pack, use the little elephant one.

SILAS: Yeah, Daddy, use the elephant. The big one makes my yogurt frozen. But not banana yogurt, I want the other kind.

JASON (walks to the refrigerator, tripping on a toy en route. He opens the fridge, but finds no yogurt): We don't have any . . .

LINDSAY (cutting off Jason): Never mind. I'll do it. You just find Arlo's green socks.

JASON (walking around aimlessly in a daze): I think they must be in the car.

LINDSAY: Ugh, okay, I'll find the green socks. You make the tuna fish. Oh, and make sure you put some apples in his lunch too or something. He has to eat fruit every day or he won't poop.

SILAS: But what about my egg? I'm starving!

JASON: I'm trying to make your lunch.

LINDSAY (cutting off Jason): Never mind. I'll make lunch, you make the egg.

ARLO: WANT MY GWEEN SOCKS!

SILAS: Daddy, I think Arlo wants his green socks. (saunters into the living room and starts doing a puzzle)

JASON: Yes, I gathered that. Thanks, buddy. We have to leave for school in five minutes.

ARLO: No Silas! Dat Arlo puzzle.

LINDSAY: Silas, can you stop doing Arlo's puzzle and get your shoes on?

SILAS: OH FINE!

JASON: Do you still want your egg?

CUT TO SUNROOM: Arlo paces, holding three puzzle pieces while chanting, "Gween socks, gween socks."

CUT TO DOORWAY: Silas and Jason are ready to go. Jason holds a plate with an egg on it as Silas scoops it into his mouth with a spoon.

LINDSAY: You're going to be late!

15 MINUTES LATER: Jason returns from dropping off Silas at school to find that everything is calm and Arlo is wearing his green socks.

BLACK SCREEN: It's only 8:30 A.M.

END

How to Threaten Your Children Effectively

The important thing to know here is that any sort of punishment you drop on your kids involves taking away something they love—be it free time, coloring, drawing on their sibling, or television-watching— which is really a punishment for you because when they're engaged in the activities they enjoy, you get some peace and quiet. Here are some of the mistakes I've made in this regard and some ways I could have handled them better.

THREAT #1: "If you ask to watch TV one more time, I'm tossing it out the window."

PROBLEM: There are many. For starters, what the hell am *I* going to do without a television? Also, I live in a nice community, and throwing things out the window would result in extreme ostracism by my neighbors.

REVISION: "If you ask to watch TV one more time, I'll wander into the kitchen and stand there eating all the brownies until I figure out if I'm willing to distract you from the television by enthusiastically suggesting that we play a nice round of Zingo!"

THREAT #2: "Brush your teeth, or they'll turn green."

PROBLEM: Kids really don't care at all about what happens in the future unless by "the future" you mean the next eight seconds.

REVISION: "If you don't brush your teeth, they'll get this weird orange film on them. Look at your little brother's teeth. See that stuff on them? He has that because he's three years old and screams if we try to put a toothbrush in his mouth. Also, if you don't brush, you'll have to go to the dentist, and even though I've said his office is *awesome* and *super fun* and *a place that gives you stickers*, it actually sucks, and you want to avoid it at all costs."

THREAT #3: "Either you get dressed right now, or you're never getting dressed again."

PROBLEM: Not letting your child wear clothes is a red flag to child services. It also breaks your heart when after ten days they start begging you to let them get dressed.

REVISION: "If you don't get dressed, I'm going to become very still and stare out at the window until you ask me if I'm okay."

THREAT #4: "If you don't let me cut your fingernails, they're going to slice your face open."

PROBLEM: Now my three-year-old thinks his hands are weapons and is destined to develop some kind of *Edward Scissorhands* complex.

REVISION: "I want to cut your fingernails because I bite mine incessantly—to the point where there's nothing left to bite—and every time I see your beautiful, young, creamy, long fingernails, I fantasize about waiting until you're asleep and chewing them off. I'm not proud of that, and I know it's not okay, but luckily there's an easy fix."

THREAT #5: "If you don't stop crying, I'm going to cry too."

PROBLEM: I can't cry on cue, so in the unlikely event that he calls my bluff, I'll be stuck staring at him, mired in the quicksand of my lie or, even worse, trying to fake-cry. The only thing more disconcerting to a child than seeing his father weep is realizing what a terrible actor his father is. "Daddy, is that really how you cry? You look silly." Me: "This is totally how I cry. Does it look unnatural?"

REVISION: "If you don't stop crying, I'll ask you over and over again why you're crying, even though you can't catch your breath long enough to answer me. I'll hold you in my arms and say things like, 'It's going to be okay, sweet boy,' but I'll be rolling my eyes, since it's completely ridiculous to cry for fifteen minutes because the cat stepped on your foot."

THREAT #6: "If you go to bed with dirty feet, mushrooms will grow on them overnight."

PROBLEM: Silas is only five and, like most other kids his age, finds mushrooms to be the most disgusting thing in the universe. Now I fear that he'll obsessively start washing his feet like he's at the Ganges river cleansing for an afternoon prayer.

REVISION: "Going to bed with dirty feet will . . . actually, you know what? It doesn't matter *at all*. Fact is, I just feel like I'm not very helpful around here sometimes, and one of the only things I can do to contribute is to keep you clean. So, when you go to bed, I don't feel like I've been a good father if your feet . . . wait, are you still awake?"

Parenting the Firstborn vs. the Second-Born*

After our first child, we still had energy and hope. We were committed to providing him with the best upbringing imaginable. But then the second one came along and everything fell apart. We also realized that all that amazing parenting we were doing was as unnecessary as rotating the tires on our car.

Food

FIRST KID: All homemade in special baby food-processor. Quinoa! Spinach! Sweet potatoes!

SECOND KID: Crackers.

Bed

FIRST KID: Crib that Daddy put together himself while Mommy yelled at him.

SECOND KID: Mommy's bed. Daddy now has his own room with a mattress on the floor surrounded by dirty socks.

Clothes

FIRST KID: One hundred percent organic cotton. Some even made of bamboo?

SECOND KID: His brother's old clothes.

---

* or third, or fourth, or . . . you have five? What the hell's the matter with you?

Parties

FIRST KID: In our backyard with a piñata hanging from the Japanese maple.

SECOND KID: Pizza on the floor.

Bathing

FIRST KID: Every night in a special bathtub that's just the right size. Hand washed with a soft cloth or silky sponge.

SECOND KID: Twice a week. Swimming pools count.

Nighttime Routine

FIRST KID: Swaddled in a Miracle Blanket. "Baby Beluga" sung to him. Asleep by 7:30 P.M.

SECOND KID: Falls asleep on the sofa with mom's boob in his mouth at 10:30 P.M.

Friends

FIRST KID: Play groups, mommy and baby get-togethers in the park!

SECOND KID: His brother's friends.

Toys

FIRST KID: All handmade out of wood. Mostly Swedish.

SECOND KID: Paper, crayons, the boxes his older brother's toys came in.

TV Rules

FIRST KID: *Baby Einstein* and *Sesame Street* only. Two 23-minute shows per day.

SECOND KID: Has his own Netflix account.

Babysitter

FIRST KID: A wonderful woman named Sarah, whom he loves and will cherish for the rest of his life.

SECOND KID: Doesn't have one. We never go out.

Shoes

FIRST KID: Something European with an umlaut in its name.

SECOND KID: Old muddy shoes with faded umlaut and missing sole insert.

Potty Training

FIRST KID: Diapers, then pull-ups, then some kind of training underwear, then underwear.

SECOND KID: Might crap in a diaper until college.

And you know what's interesting? They're both equally awesome.

What Annoying Parents Say . . . and the Truth

I can't help but be impossibly annoyed by competitive parenting. I would much rather hear about your daughter barfing on her gerbil than how well she can roll her R's when speaking Spanish. Here are some of the more grotesquely braggy statements I've overheard, followed by what I think (or at least hope) is the reality of situation.

"My son just loves to eat raw chard."
REALITY: He accidentally ate it once because he thought it was some kind of lime-flavored candy. Kid cried himself to sleep while parent updated Facebook status to "BAXTER LOVES CHARD."

"Our kids don't like TV. In fact, we don't even have one in the house!"
REALITY: Their kids watch videos on the computer and iPad incessantly. Probably more than they would if there was a TV in the house.

"Our son's favorite country is Liberia."
REALITY: He said "Liberia" once, but what he meant was Siberia because he'd just watched (on the iPad) the episode of *Super Friends* where Lex Luthor traps Superman in a Siberian ice block. The kid's favorite country is actually "I don't know. Is a country the same thing as a mountain? Because my favorite mountain is Canada."

"Well, we recently discovered that gluten . . .
blah . . . gas . . . IQ score . . ."

(sorry, I tend to lose focus after hearing the word "gluten")

REALITY: The parents are gluten-intolerant, or think they are, and don't want it in the house because they don't trust themselves not to eat it. Full disclosure: I might be allergic to gluten, but will never find out because my love of bread far exceeds the discomfort and hassle of farting and being tired all the time. Of course, my karmic fate for this joke will be that my kids are gluten-intolerant and I become that which I mock.

"You should switch to cloth diapers."

REALITY: They bought two hundred dollars-worth of cloth diapers and regret it horribly, but they're stuck because they told everyone they cared about the environment. Now they want everyone else to ruin their washing machines, just like they did.

"My child slept through the night at four months old!"

REALITY: Their child sleeps through the night because a) they have a night nurse who's nice enough not to tell them when their child awakens at night or b) they put on noise-canceling earphones and "sleep trained" him. There's nothing wrong with either of those, but stop telling half-truths and making the rest of us feel inadequate because a three-year-old sleeps in between us.

Taking a Bath
with Your Child

*Sometimes the only way you can get your kid to
take a bath is by saying, "Do you want Daddy
to get in too?" Now, unless you have a hot tub inside
your house, which is actually against the law north
of the Mason–Dixon Line, normal bathtubs
are generally too small for an adult and a child.
I'm also extremely tall, so there's some added
difficulty there. It might be slightly easier for you,
but these are the things I've learned.*

1. **USE LESS WATER.** You are a giant creature (no offense) and you displace a great deal of water.

2. **GET IN FIRST.** Your child needs to see the one square foot of space between your legs where he will have to sit. Comfy!

3. **THIS BATH IS NOT FOR YOU.** You will not get clean from this experience. In fact, you will likely have to take a shower later to wash off all the bubble scum, toothpaste, glue, glitter, candle wax, temporary tattoos . . . look, my kid likes to bring stuff in the bath, including his father.

4. **USE A SPACE HEATER.** You're going to be freezing. The kid thinks all water is too hot, plus you won't be able to get more than 20 percent of your body submerged, so you'll be sitting in eight inches of tepid water shivering to death. It's like ice fishing except you're naked and accompanied by a naked child, and you don't have fishing gear—never mind.

5. **HAVE TOWELS READY.** I'm sorry, but there's nothing I can say that will prevent you from making this mistake every single time. If your house is like mine, there is never a towel hanging on the rack. You won't remember that, though. So, like me, you'll get out and you'll get your child out, only to realize you haven't got a drying device. No, you cannot use the space heater. With your child standing in place dripping wet, you'll walk to the hall closet BUTT NAKED, probably slipping on the wood floor and pulling a neck muscle. When you come back, the child is gone—off streaking through the house, diaperless and cackling, and making everything damp.

Safe Places to Eat Cookies

Parents need to indulge in cookie-eating binges. Usually we're able to hold off until the kids are asleep, but sometimes, the urge hits us when they're awake and totally aware that there are cookies in the house. Just because they've had their recommended daily allowance doesn't mean Mom or Dad can't pound the rest of the bag. The trick is to make sure you don't let them see you do it. I know it's embarrassing—infantilizing even—but the best thing you can do is hide. Choose your place wisely. I recommend the following.

1. In the garage
2. Behind the shed
3. Inside the shed
4. In the shower
5. In the shower with the water on (slightly more effective)
6. In the boiler room
7. On the toilet
8. Under the covers in a dark room with the door locked

9. Inside your car parked in the driveway

10. Right in front of your child, while chanting "COOKIE ONLY FOR DADDY. COOKIE ONLY FOR DADDY." (This never works.)

11. Really anywhere, as long as you're crying while eating them

12. From the inside of a ski mask. Instructions: Fill ski mask with cookies, put on ski mask, open mouth, chew furiously, hope for the best.

13. You're probably thinking, "Hey, Jason, what about the closet?" Rookie mistake. They always find you there because that's *their* secret place for eating cookies (and sometimes for peeing).

What We've Googled

After being a parent for over five years,
here are some phrases my family may or may not
have searched for on Google.

1. Dried puke in slipper contagious?

2. 55kaw0jADHSASŚ*BOB*THE*BUILDER*iPAD*
   MOMMY*;;,,,,,nb

3. Babies in African villages happier?

4. New parents + frequency of sex + normal

5. Toddler won't wear coat

6. Lack of REM sleep and IQ related?

7. Younger sibling bites older sibling normal?

8. Canadian pharmacy untraceable P.O. box felony?

9. Is 40 too old to wear jeggings?

10. Angry Birds Rio level 8-15 cheat

11. Images: "kids having fun at dentist"

12. "Nipple confusion" myth?

13. Dad poker night New Jersey over by 9 P.M.

The Arithmetic of Parenting

FULL DISCLOSURE: I misspelled "arithmetic" five times before finally getting it right. But that's spelling, not math. I'm very skilled at "math things." I believe that there's an equation all parents use while watching their children play (albeit subconsciously) to determine whether they're needed. Think of it as a Pythagorean theorem for caregivers.

$$\frac{(\text{LI} \times \text{SI})}{\text{CSC}} = \text{KC}$$

LI stands for "likelihood of injury" scale from 1 to 100.

SI is "severity of injury" scale from 1 to 20.

CSC is the parent's "current state of comfort" scale from 1 to 100.

KC stands for "kinetic concern," which is a variable I've created to measure the degree to which a parent is willing to expend energy in order to help his or her children. Anything above 1.0 should cause the caregiver to go into motion.

Let's use an example. Imagine you're lying in the hammock watching your young child play on the monkey bars. Because he's accustomed to these monkey bars, there is a very low likelihood of injury (LI). But, since the bars are so high off the ground, there's an elevated severity of injury (SI). And, obviously, since you're in the hammock, the current state of comfort (CSC) is quite high. The equation would look like this:

$$\frac{(5 \times 14)}{95} = 0.74$$

With a kinetic concern (KC) score of less than 1.0, it's perfectly reasonable for you to remain sedentary. But what if the monkey bars had been even higher off the ground, and you were sitting on a chair instead of lying in a hammock? The likelihood of injury (LI) would remain the same, but with an increased severity of injury (SI) coupled with a decreased current state of comfort (CSC), the kinetic concern (KC) value would be much higher.

$$\frac{(5 \times 17)}{55} = 1.55$$

This is a clear call to action, and everyone knows it.

There is one frightening and common situation in which this equation fails us: when our children are out of our sight and very quiet. If LI and SI are both unknown, and only CSC is observable, can we still solve for KC? Let's try.

$$\frac{(LI \times SI)}{75} = \text{SYNTAX ERROR.}$$
$$\text{VC Required!}$$

Don't panic. According to Dr. Spock, VC is an acronym for "verbal confirmation." In this case, the course of action is still relatively simple: Yell, "It's awfully quiet down there. Is everything okay?" If you don't receive a VC after three attempts, assume LI is over 80 and SI is at least 18. This means that even with a CSC of 100, the KC will be over 1.0, so you should leap off the toilet and make sure the kids aren't in the gross part of the basement playing with a crossbow.

Operation Roommate

Here's the psychologically complex eight-step process my son used to trick me into sleeping in his bed with him. I encourage you to watch for the warning signs that your kid might be attempting something similar.

STEP 1. ESTABLISH NEED. Wake frequently, causing your father to go from a dead sleep to a full-on sprint at least fifteen times a night. You're the firstborn, so your parents still freak out anytime you cry. Use this to your advantage.

STEP 2. CONVERGENCE. After twelve consecutive nights, your parents will start putting you to sleep in their bed where you'll stay all night. This is only the first rest stop on a long road. Remember, the idea is to get your father in *your* bed. So pay attention; the following steps require patience and cunning.

STEP 3. THE BLUFF. A few weeks after achieving convergence, you must spontaneously offer to sleep in your own bed. This might be hard, but your parents will probably buy you a cake and let you drink all the chocolate milk you want, so it's pretty much worth it. Plus, it's only temporary—*you're only doing this so your mommy can get pregnant again.* Operation Roommate requires a sibling.

STEP 4. DIVIDE AND CONQUER. Soon, the pregnancy causes sleeping problems for Mommy and Daddy, and they decide (well, mostly she'll decide) it would be best if she had the whole king-size bed to herself. Daddy cooperates and goes to sleep in the guest room. *You now have them exactly where you want them.*

STEP 5. STAY COMMITTED. This is a tough one, and I don't have any words of wisdom here other than "Be strong." For eight months, you wake only once during the night. Your dad will remain steadfast in his commitment to nocturnal independence. Don't worry, because it will all come together.

STEP 6. INCREASE INTENSITY. The moment has arrived. Your brother is here and all hell has broken loose. There's a furious, hairless, shrieking thing in your mommy's room. Daddy will offer to help her, but he's sent back to his bachelor room where a scarf serves as a lampshade. He's thirty-nine years old. You must seize this moment. Increase the frequency of your wakings to four per night. Make sure you're loud enough to consistently awaken your brother. In order to quiet the 1 A.M., 3 A.M., 4 A.M., and 5 A.M. foghorns, your daddy will come into your room and occasionally stay there.

STEP 7. LEVERAGE EMPATHY. Now, do you know what empathy is? The only thing you need to understand is that it makes grown-ups weak. Use it against them. When Daddy reads to you at night, ask in your sweetest, most innocent voice, "Daddy, will you stay in here and sleep with me all night?" You must cry softly each time he says, "No, sorry, sweetie, Daddy sleeps in the room with no heat." After one week, your father will relent and Operation Roommate has nearly reached fruition. It's been a long, hard battle.

STEP 8. PAMPER THE PRISONER. The first night of sharing a bed, you must do everything you can to avoid waking your father. The next day everyone will be happier than they've been in months and your mom will say, "Jace, you should probably just sleep in there all the time, right?" Congratulations, young one, you have successfully made your father sleep in a full-size bed with you every night. You broke him. Mornings will now be just like summer camp. You'll wake up and innocently say, "Daddy? Are you awake?" and then you'll talk about comic books for twenty-five minutes before heading into the main lodge to eat Lucky Charms with the other campers.

Why I'm Fat Now

We're all getting fat; mostly due to age, but also because we don't have time to make good meals for ourselves. I've sat down to "eat a proper meal" in my own home about a dozen times in the last five years. The day described below is much more common, and exemplifies something I like to call "The County Jail Vending Machine Diet."

8:15 A.M.
One piece of multigrain toast with butter and three cups of coffee (reasonable start)

12:30 P.M.
One and a half cupcakes, one espresso, one iced coffee (I think I might drink too much coffee. HI, HOW ARE YOU! I'M FINE! I LIKE TO CLEAN STUFF AND CALL PEOPLE ON THE TELEPHONE.)

1:30 P.M.
Two Popsicles

2:00 P.M.
My legs begin to quiver and I am on the verge of a Victorian-era fainting spell. My blood is 75 percent corn syrup and I need real food. Commence refugee panic eating.

2:03 P.M.

A chicken-finger sandwich with mayonnaise, three heaping spoonfuls of peanut butter and more Wheat Thins than I could possibly count. Oh, and a big glass of water. I feel a little better but I still "take to my bed" for about twenty minutes. My wife suggests I may be overreacting, but my hands were shaking. Maybe my blood sugar was low?

2:30 P.M.

A handful of jelly beans

9:30 P.M.

A medium frozen yogurt with fruity bears (a heartfelt apology to all men for that one)

11:15 P.M.

A small bag of barbecue potato chips and a Charleston Chew (because sometimes I like to party like a 1920s hobo)

I woke the next morning and did what I needed to do to feel healthy again: I went to the nice grocery store and stared at the vitamins and colon cleansers.

Signs That You're a Bad Parent

Again, there's no permanent damage here, but at the same time, if you nod to more than, say, half of these things, you should really step up your game.

1. Your child claims his favorite flavor is purple.

2. He refers to the dining room wall as his canvas.

3. When he gives hugs, he says, "Oh yeah, gimme some sugar!"

4. He knows all the characters on *Game of Thrones*.

5. His favorite color is chocolate.

6. Having never been potty trained, he's now too big for regular diapers and must wear Depends.

7. His bedtime is "Whenever Mommy finishes her cigarette."

8. He tells his friends that toast is a fruit.

9. When you ask, "Now, what do we do if the cops come to the door?" he answers, "Flush Daddy's stash."

10. Other kids aren't allowed to play at your house.

11. His litter box is always full.

12. When asked at school, "What's your favorite thing about weekends?" he screams, "FUDGE FOR DINNER!"

13. He makes the best Tom Collins you've ever tasted.

14. The pounding on the attic floor no longer keeps you up at night.

Rules for Power Outages

Long power outages, like those experienced after a hurricane, can be used to your advantage. Instead of you telling them "no TV," now the bad news is coming directly from the universe. It's an opportunity to live by the rules of pioneers. Run with it.

1. Bedtime is at "sundown."

2. No talking to Daddy while he's chopping wood (or running a power strip into the house from the car).

3. No pestering Mommy while she's churning the evening butter (i.e., making instant pudding for dinner).

4. It's the responsibility of children to frolic on command.

5. Whenever a child asks, "Where's Daddy?" an acceptable answer is, "Off hunting for your dinner! Now get back to whittling a new spoon for your brother."

6. You can respond to any complaint of "I'm tired" with, "Only children with Juniper Fever get tired. Now go out and see if the chickens laid any eggs."

Those all seem like a drag for the kids. Luckily, there are plenty of things you can say yes to now—but only during power outages when survival depends on the participation of every family member. The minimum age for all these activities is four.

1. Lighting a candle
2. Making coffee
3. Not bathing
4. Hiking half a mile to stand in line for gas
5. Operating a sump pump
6. Milking a cow
7. Looting
8. Putting new shoes on a horse
9. Dressing up like Oliver Twist to charm old man Gildernhorn into offering us some of his clean water

COMMUNICATE!
COMMUNICATE!
COMMUNICATE!

Young children rarely make sense, and when they do, what they're saying is almost always something totally irrational. The quicker you accept this, the happier and more harmonious your home life will be.

Understanding Your Children

Your kid speaks in code, making effective communication quite difficult. Luckily, I'm here to decipher that code for you.

"Just one more time."

TRANSLATION: Keep doing this until you injure yourself or I cry.

"I'm not hungry."

TRANSLATION: I'm extremely hungry, but there's something more pressing at the moment than eating. But when I'm done, YOU BETTER HAVE SOME FOOD READY!

"I'm tired."

TRANSLATION: I'm bored.

"It's too sunny out!"

TRANSLATION: I'm tired.

"I love dancing!"

TRANSLATION: I have to pee.

"Jake hit me."

TRANSLATION: All I did was kick and bite Jake
and then he pushed my hand away.

"I don't like Jake."

TRANSLATION: Jake has a play date with Ryan.

"This food is too hot."

TRANSLATION: This food is one degree
above room temperature.

"I LOVE SCHOOL."

TRANSLATION: We had cupcakes at school today.

"I can't find my shoes."

TRANSLATION: I haven't looked for my shoes.

"This milk tastes like socks."

TRANSLATION: This milk reminds me of the time I ate a sock.

"I *really* need Mommy."

TRANSLATION: Can you get Mommy out of the shower
so I can show her the new way I can lick the sofa?

"My favorite color is red."

TRANSLATION: Mommy's favorite color is red
and I want to be just like her.

Self-Help from a Three-Year-Old

Having kids isn't all that bad when you realize how much you can learn from them. We all need that special someone, be it a guru, a sun god, a moon god, or a psychiatrist. Look no further than your toddler. Following his or her example will lead to the Valley of Enlightenment.

1. Challenge yourself every day. Try climbing the stairs carrying two soccer balls while wearing your father's shoes. Remember, failure *is* an option.

2. De-clutter! Start by throwing all your dishes in the garbage. After that, I suggest toothbrushes and important paperwork.

3. Pee on the floor and stomp in it like a puddle. You'll be shocked how much better you feel.

4. Whether the glass is half empty or half full is irrelevant if you dump it out on the sofa. You're welcome!

5. If you're feeling aggressive, or just bored, scream in a cat's face.

6. Don't ever be afraid to hand someone an ice cube while they're on the toilet.

7. Pound on a computer keyboard. Do you feel super-productive, now? I thought so.

8. If you fall down, stay down. Someone will pick you up eventually.

9. Have you learned to delete things off the DVR yet? DO IT. It's AwWwWwEsOmE.

10. Seize the day and the night and the middle of the night and the early morning. Seize everything, y'all! Never stop seizing stuff.

11. Tired of looking at yourself in the mirror? So was I until I met my friend *permanent marker*. FACE TATTOOS ARE RAD.

12. This might be a tough one, but you gotta trust me: Poop in the tub. It's surreal. Tell Daddy you "did a number 12." He won't laugh, but that doesn't mean it's not funny!

13. Live in the moment because there is nothing else. Seriously, there isn't. Not that I'm aware, of at least.

14. If you're gonna run, do it at top speed, man. Life is too short to walk in the mall.

Use Your Best
Kindergarten Spelling

One of my five-year-old son's assignments in kindergarten is to keep a "night write journal." The kids are instructed to use their "kindergarten spelling," which means, "Just do your best!" These are some of my favorite entries.

I woosht shoos aool day

WHAT I THOUGHT IT SAID: I washed shoes all day (poor kid)

WHAT IT ACTUALLY SAID: I watched [TV] shows all day (someone call social services)

I went to a Proortyll

WHAT I THOUGHT IT SAID: I went to a pterodactyl

WHAT IT ACTUALLY SAID: I went to a party

I plaed with mt 6amoo

WHAT I THOUGHT IT SAID: He played with his friend 6amoo (weird name!) which is apparently a mountain (also weird)

WHAT IT ACTUALLY SAID: I played with my grandma

iam grouch whe my braurttist me

WHAT I THOUGHT IT SAID: Something about a grouchy bratwurst

WHAT IT ACTUALLY SAID: I am grouchy when my brother hits me

I Plyd way it was Fan

WHAT I THOUGHT IT SAID: . . . ? ? ? ? . . .
WHAT IT ACTUALLY SAID: I played Wii. It was fun.

I goat poops els

WHAT I THOUGHT IT SAID: I'm a goat that poops eels? (horrifying)
WHAT IT ACTUALLY SAID: I got Popsicles

I loot at noo hoasis

WHAT I THOUGHT IT SAID: I looted no horses (good boy!)
WHAT IT ACTUALLY SAID: I looked at new houses

I jopt in a pad. I woct Ho Min ve ran

WHAT I THOUGHT IT SAID: Something about running around
Ho Chi Min City with an iPad?
WHAT IT ACTUALLY SAID: I jumped in a puddle. I walked home
in the rain.

If I had the big st icecream I wad edit olap

WHAT I THOUGHT IT SAID: If I had big street ice cream I would
edit [a programming language I've never heard of]
WHAT IT ACTUALLY SAID: If I had the biggest ice cream I would
eat it all up.

I had aeastreg hat

WHAT I THOUGHT IT SAID: He ate a bizarre Scandinavian hat?
WHAT IT ACTUALLY SAID: I had an Easter egg hunt

How Toddlers Tell You They're Hungry

For reasons even evolutionary biologists don't understand, young children are incapable of simply saying they're hungry. Instead, they . . .

1. Throw a shoe at the TV

2. Bite a puzzle piece

3. Rip all the petals off a flower

4. Spend ten silent minutes putting stickers on the refrigerator

5. Tear up their brother's wizard hat

6. Obsessively take off and put on their socks

7. Try to cut their own hair

8. Fall asleep at 6 P.M. while chanting, "I'm not hungry"

9. Disappear, and then resurface without pants on

10. Break the world record for "decibels achieved while playing the Elmo flute"

Then again, these behaviors might be his ways of telling you he's ...

1. Tired

2. Hot

3. Bored

4. Not hungry

5. Thirsty

6. Itchy

7. Not thirsty

8. Gassy

9. In need of a haircut

10. Experiencing an existential crisis

Kids are confusing.

Car Talk

Car rides are boring—even the ones that last four minutes. Though kids usually have a decent time, these are some of the things they like to argue over when the trip is longer than three minutes.

1. Whether we're going fast or slow

2. Where we're going

3. Why we're going there

4. When we're going to be there

5. Who will get out first when we get there

6. What the temperature is outside

7. What season it is

8. Whether the windows should be up or down

9. Why the windows don't go all the way down in the back

10. Who gets which car seat

11. Who owns the strip of fabric between their car seats

12. Who owns the car

13. Who has more crackers

14. Who's the louder singer

15. Whether or not it's sunny out

16. Whose tongue is bigger

17. Who can kick the chair in front of them the hardest

18. Why Daddy is so quiet

Building a Fort with a Five-Year-Old

To help you understand these mysterious creatures even better, I recorded what I believe to be the thought process of an average five-year-old boy over the course of about five minutes around 6:30 P.M. while doing his favorite thing.

1. Umm, what are the cushions doing on the sofa when they could be made into an awesome fort?

2. No, it's never too late to build a fort. What's wrong with you?

3. Wait, WHAT are you doing starting with that cushion?

4. DO YOU KNOW ANYTHING ABOUT FORTS?!???!!

5. Where's Mommy? She knows how to build a fort.

6. No, it's NOT going to fall down if I put . . .

7. Oops, you were right.

8. This fort is lame. It needs more pillows.

9. No, you go upstairs and get them.

10. I have to pee.

11. Hmm, but what about the fort?

12. Stop asking me if I have to pee! And start helping me build this fort!

13. Okay, I peed. Does that mean you will start understanding how forts work?

14. Oh my God! Did you really just use the back love seat cushion as a wall? Okay, I had no idea what I was dealing with here.

15. Should we start from the beginning? A fort has four walls and . . .

16. NO I'M NOT HUNGRY! I JUST WANT A FORT.

17. You know what question you should ask? "Hey son, how do I build a fort?"

18. Oh good, you used the big cushion for the wall. Somebody's a good listener.

19. Wait, though, there's this identical cushion from the other side of the sofa that should go there instead.

20. Umm, because I know more about forts than you, that's why.

21. You're right, that shouldn't be how it is. Unfortunately, I have a dad who knows very little about forts.

22. Okay, I like that.

23. Oh, impressive.

24. VERY NICE!

25. Okay, we need a top.

26. No, not "like a tapestry or something." I don't even know what a tapestry is, but there's no way it's a decent fort roof.

27. We put the red blanket on top and THEN the tapestry. How is that not obvious?

28. Does that look flat to you? You know saggy fort roofs make me have to pee, right? So . . . why would you do that?

29. Don't be sad. It's just a stupid fort.

30. I'm sorry. You're a good fort builder. Yes, seriously (not).

31. Okay, now it needs a door.

32. Huh? I thought you would know.

33. Oh, good call. Okay, I'm gonna climb in. No, no, it's fine, trust me.

34. Little help? This fort just collapsed on me.

35. Please rebuild the fort exactly like it was before while I lie here and drink milk.

36. No, that's already not right.

37. Well, for one, there was no steeple on the last fort.

38. What's the longest book in the house? Cool, I wanna read that before bed.

A Three-Year-Old
Searches for His Shoes

*As a bonus, here's the thought process of a typical
three-year-old as he searches for his shoes.*

1. Those my socks?

2. Looks like a red mouse.

3. Is that a red mouse?

4. Definitely not my socks.

5. Oh look, the chimney broom.

6. I'm hungry.

7. Umm, where's Mommy?

8. Where's Daddy's phone?

9. Oh look, I don't have any shoes on.

10. Ah, there's Mommy. She'll know where Daddy's phone is.

11. You know what? I don't like these pants.

12. No, not those.

13. I want a different pair of pants, like, maybe a pair I don't actually have.

14. I'll put my shoes on AFTER someone orders me new pants from the computer.

15. Where are my new pants?

16. She did that computer thing so my pants should be here now.

17. What's the cat doing? DON'T TOUCH THE RED MOUSE that might actually be my socks.

18. Crackers.

19. Crackers.

20. No, different crackers.

21. I have to pee, but not in these pants.

22. New pants here yet?

23. Seriously, I have to pee.

24. Fine, I'll pee, but my pants better be here when I'm done.

25. Oh, look! THERE are my shoes! I should probably kick them under the radiator.

26. If I turn this stool upside down can I fill it with water?

27. Nope.

28. Well, the floor's already wet, so I'll just pee here.

29. Ummm, why are they looking for my shoes when they should be waiting for my new pants?

30. How the hell would I know where my shoes are? I'm three.

How Board Games End

*This is a really short one because
there are only three possible outcomes.*

Crying

Taunting followed by
an obnoxious victory dance

Someone walks away in the middle
because they're losing

*I've found this also to be true for adults
playing Pictionary.*

Oliver's Take

*Sometimes a family needs an outsider to provide a
realistic view of day-to-day operations.
Our cat, Oliver, seems to be pretty objective.*

- Jason's posture reminds me of my mother stalking a cricket—all hunched over and intense.

- Five seconds until the little one falls and cries. Five, four, three . . . oh, that was fast.

- Damn, here he comes.

- Okay, that was my eye. And my other eye. And my pancreas.

- No idea if I have a pancreas.

- Didn't even know I was aware pancreases existed. That's weird. If you say pancreas enough you'll probably start to laugh. Or not. Whatever. Sometimes I don't even know who I am.

- I'm moving to the couch for some serious downtime.

- They're talking about the color of the walls AGAIN. I told them not to do white. Did they listen? Nope! And now they're going with dark blue? Good lord, they're all going to need lithium. Here comes talk of a new sofa in three, two, one . . . bam. These people are more predictable than me with string.

🐾 Ha ha ha ha ha ha—the big one with glasses is asking the little one about bed already. Bro, it's 6:30! Why do you do that to yourself? Give it a half hour. Trust me, I'm here way more than you are.

🐾 YES, a new episode of your stupid show is on tonight. SHUT UP!!!!!!!!!! It's on MONDAYS. Should I spray the wall to remind you?

🐾 Sorry, I think I'm just hungry.

🐾 HOLY CRAP WHAT WAS THAT?

🐾 Oh God, the vacuum cleaner.

🐾 That thing! Hey vacuum, could you sound a little less like a natural disaster? Thanks.

🐾 Jesus, look at my tail. I'm a nervous wreck now. I probably look like a raccoon.

🐾 I need some alone time.

🐾 Oh great, the basement is trashed and I just stepped on something wet. Could've been juice, could've been spit. Only way to find out is to taste it. Yup, spit. Whatever. I'm out.

Needed: Hollywood Agents for Parents

Kids are soprano-voiced, bossy movie directors.
We can state our case for not going down to the basement
right now, but they're relentless in their commitment
to seeing things through. I imagine it's the same when
you're on set with Quentin Tarantino or Martin Scorsese;
they know what they want and no one's going to get
in their way. Like actors on a set, parents need good
representation, someone they can turn to when their boss
becomes unreasonable and they've lost their ability
to communicate in a calm, rational manner. Let's look
at some examples.

THE ISSUE: No matter how much you ask, and no matter how stern you sound or how loudly you yell, your kid won't stop throwing food on the floor so the cat eats it and barfs all over your new sofa. It's tough, isn't it? Is your flabbergasted tone helping the situation? Probably not. Call your agent.

AGENT: "Look, kid, I know it's funny when the cat barfs. And I'm an expert on funny because I worked on the set of *The Hangover*. Did I ever tell you that? The truth is (and don't tell your mom or dad I said this), I've loved all your work, going all the way back to the time you threw your snow boot in the toilet. You're a true icon and idol to toddlers everywhere. But the fact is, you're creating a very difficult working environment for my client and since he's the one who provides the food you're throwing, it's probably best if you cool it. At least wait until he leaves the room. Deal?"

THE ISSUE: Your kid refuses to let you change his diaper. You're chasing him around the house hunched over like Rocky trying to catch a chicken. Your back is spasming and you're moments from giving up. Do not give up! Call your agent.

AGENT: "Yo, my man! What is that smell? Righteous, bro! Heyyyyyyy, I know you're proud of what you did there and, hell, who wouldn't be? I was so proud of the way I negotiated Tom Cruise's salary for *Minority Report*. Did I ever tell you about that? Anyway, whaddya say we change those soily drawers so you can spend all of that creative energy on your next diaper-fillin' project?"

I'm going to stop myself there. It occurs to me that these "agents" I speak of already exist and they're called "grandfathers."

The Stages of Parenting

*If these look familiar, it's because they are
also the seven stages of grief.*

1. **SHOCK AND DENIAL**

   Let's say, for instance, that you ask your child a question
   and they simply stare back at you blankly. You ask
   it again, but are met with the same response. Because
   you want to believe your child is good, you assume
   they must not have heard you, perhaps because they
   have peas stuck in their ears. You make your request
   yet again, only this time loudly enough to remove
   any doubt. Nothing.

2. **PAIN AND GUILT**

   The parent realizes the child hasn't listened and,
   in fact, might be actively ignoring them. It hurts
   deeply, but, in the end, the parent understands that
   something they've done has caused their child to
   behave this way.

3. **ANGER AND BARGAINING**

   In the face of pain and guilt over what they believe
   to be an increasingly dysfunctional relationship,
   frustration begins bubbling to the surface. It's a

completely natural reaction in this stage for the parent to become angry and sometimes yell at the child. The child might cry or return the angry yell, at which point the parent returns briefly to the guilt stage. Because of this, the parent will apologize and bribe the child to stop crying.

4. **DEPRESSION, REFLECTION, AND LONELINESS**

Regardless of the outcome, the parent will experience some sadness over how the situation was handled. Thinking back, they understand this is a bad pattern and an overwhelming sense of doubt about their parenting skills sets in. When the child naps, or goes off to school, the parent is left alone realizing that someday that same child will be leaving for college.

5. **THE UPWARD TURN**

"Next time I will handle this differently. They grow up too fast to spend so much time struggling with them over stupid stuff." This is a very common thought at this stage. A new energy is directed toward improving the future. The parent/child relationship appears to be headed in a more positive direction. Familial bliss has returned, and the future seems ripe with family vacations filled with laughter and cuddling.

6. **RECONSTRUCTION AND WORKING THROUGH**

With everyone so happy, the parent does all they can to ensure things stay that way. The parent might attempt to set up systems through which rewards are given for good behavior. The child seems excited about this new game. A new kind of relationship arises, and both parties express their commitment to it.

7. **ACCEPTANCE AND HOPE**

Things are different now. Both parent and child are aware of this. It wasn't ideal for either of them, but each recognizes the change is necessary if harmony is to be maintained. After only a few days, however, this new structure begins to crumble, and the entire process must begin again. The parent hopes the stages will be different this time, but they almost never are. They once again are shocked and enter a state of denial when the child appears to have unlearned all the lessons of the previous few days. All the parent can do is try again, and believe that eventually harmony will stick around.

Arlo's Letter to Santa

If my three-year-old son had the verbal skills and self-awareness to make a Christmas list, I imagine it might read something like this.

Dear Santa Claus (weird name by the way. You'd think since you're so big with kids, you'd stay away from all those *S* sounds. You know we're bad at them, right?),

Here's the stuff I want. And by "want," I mean "NEED."

1. My own dishwasher so I can use the door as a trampoline (honestly, there's something about the springiness that I haven't been able to replicate anywhere else).

2. If you have control over laws and stuff like that (you must have sway at least, right?), make pants illegal. I bet that one's on other kids' lists too.

3. How many lollipops do you have up there in Greenland? *GIVE THEM ALL TO ME.* (That was supposed to be a scary demon voice. Not sure how fonts work, but that's what I was trying to do. Really really really want lots of lollipops. Like, at least eight. K?)

4. Rip-away clothes. Not sure if that's what they're called, but I want a shirt that, when I tug on the front of it, it comes off.

5. A JACKHAMMER!

6. A rabbit. In case you're out of those, I can live with a squirrel or buffalo. All seem neat and fun.

7. A Jet Ski. Have you SEEN those things?!!!!

8. Ninety minutes of foot reflexology. (No idea what this is, but it seems to be popular with my mom and her friends, so I figure I'll give it a shot.)

9. POPCORN and lots of it. Cheese popcorn is preferable, but I could also go with kettle or caramel. Actually, just get me ten of those combo buckets. I was going to put this first, but didn't want to come on too strong right off the bat.

10. A pommel horse.

Love,
Arlo

From Arlo to Silas

He's too young to talk much, but my three-year-old has some things he'd like to communicate to his five-year-old brother.

Silas,

I have to make it quick because I need to get my diaper off and show everyone how awesome I am at taking a whiz. When was the last time you watched me pee, by the way? After that, I'm gonna get mom to hold me up and name all the stuff in the fridge. Until then, I wanna rap about a few issues, cool?

First off, you're rad. I know I'm just a dude who knocks stuff over and jumps on you, but I'm only three, man! Give me a year at least to get it together. I can't even count so well yet.

I do what I do, you know? I'm a havoc-wreaker and a room-wrecker. That's my game.

You've been there and done that already. Throwing peas is snoozeville for you. I respect that. I don't need you to come down to my level. I'm not asking you to regress, but you gotta understand, I don't have many friends and when I do see kids my age, I get so excited it freaks them out.

Here's what I'm trying to say: I'm gonna be around for a long time, so like, maybe we should start figuring out how to do stuff together. You like Play-Doh, right? See? I LOVE Play-Doh. There's one thing right there we can do together. What if, like, you made a Play-Doh pizza and I pretended to eat it and we both laughed? Is that something you'd be into? I gotta be honest here, I would probably slap the pizza while you're making it, but don't get frustrated and stop. It's part of being with me.

Maybe that can be my job in the pizza making. I can be the slapper. As soon as you think it's done, I hit it and mess it all up and then eat it. HILARIOUS, riiiiiiight?

Here's another possibility. Do you think the cats are weird? ME TOO! We can totally do weird stuff to the cats together. Have you seen me lie on top of the orange one? He doesn't even try to move. I don't know what's wrong with him, but he just sits there and waits for me to get off him, and I think I'm getting pretty heavy. I don't really know how we could do that together, but maybe you could laugh while I do it instead of trying to pull me off? I know you're trying to impress Mom and Dad and probably save the cat's life, but we're brothers, and that's way more important than Mom or Dad or cats, right?

Here are some other things we might be able to jam at together. Due to time issues, I'm just gonna list them. If any of these seem cool to you, let me know.

1. See how long we can hold a piece of ice in our hands

2. Play inside the car while it's off

3. Take all the books off the shelves in the basement and jump on them

4. Explore the creepy laundry room

5. Pee in the cat litter (I've totally been doing this when no one's looking. It's great.)

Okay, I'm off to whiz. (In the toilet. Ha.)

Love,
Arlo

P.S. We're gonna do "puffy" later, right? That thing where Dad throws up the fitted sheet and we jump on it when it lands? It's my favorite part of the day.

THIS IS RIDICULOUS
THIS IS AMAZING

A child does not show his love
through required acts of giving, but instead
through the honesty of his spirit.

—Me, making up a Deepak Chopra quote

The Seven Stages
of a Tantrum

Tantrums don't come out of nowhere. Actually,
they do, but after they start they tend to go through
seven distinct stages.

STAGE 1: It begins with an ominous, guttural moan.
It's short and if you aren't paying attention, you might
think it's your dog snoring.

STAGE 2: The moan becomes louder, with fewer lows
and more highs until it's full-on shrieking. You can hear
the word "want" over and over again, but the rest of the
sentence is unintelligible yammering.

STAGE 3: Generally this is where the parent steps
in and tries to figure out what the child wants. This is
always a mistake because the child desperately wants
you to know, innately, what he wants at all times.
Displaying your failure to understand his every need at
every second of the day only escalates his fury.

STAGE 4: "WANT" is now accompanied by "... THING!"
This is a trap. Do not say, "What thing?" (see Stage 3).
This isn't something you're capable of solving at this
point (or ever). Tip: The "thing" is almost always a
random piece of plastic that has no meaning to anyone
but the child. Good luck finding it.

STAGE 5: This is the peak of the tantrum and is indicated by the child flopping onto the floor. FOR THE LOVE OF GOD, DO NOT TOUCH THE CHILD. Do not speak to the child either. This is a good opportunity to get some cleaning done. You're superfluous during this stage. If you do pick the child up, you must replace him in the exact same spot. An easy way to do this is to line up the trail of spit and snot on the floor with the child's nostrils and mouth. Be careful here; holding a child in this condition is like carrying a live fish around with salad tongs.

STAGE 6: You're over the hump. The child is breathing again. Now is an okay time to speak with him, for the demon has left his body. It's still not safe to touch him, but soothing words—the kind that moments ago seemed to only increase his agitation—can now do some good. But under no circumstances should you reference "THAT THING" because it can cause a relapse. You must redirect the child's attention. Suggest doing something he really enjoys, like spilling the cat's water or changing the dishwasher from the "normal" setting to "pots and pans."

STAGE 7: I call this the "honeymoon." It's over and your child wants to cuddle. He is still heaving and having trouble talking, but the crocodile tears have all dripped off his cheeks. He's sniffing repeatedly, but it's only residual snot. Hug him, squeeze him, perhaps give him a cracker, and NEVER SPEAK OF IT AGAIN.

Ridiculous Things
I've Said

*Here are a few ridiculous things that have come
out of my mouth over the course of a month as a result
of having young kids.*

1. Careful, you're getting a lot of crumbs in my hair.

2. Stop hugging your brother and finish your hot dog.

3. Don't pull anyone's skin.

4. I'll race you to the Band-Aids.

5. No climbing on the mantle.

6. Okay, then what does the Grab Monster do if he doesn't grab anything?

7. I wish they made cool jeans like that for adults.

8. Keep your penis in your pants when you're outside.

9. We SWALLOW food in this house.

10. I can't change the channel from the toilet.

11. Don't bite my shoulder.

12. Because it would probably hurt if I carried you around by your head.

13. Don't smack the flowers.

Some Fantastic
Winter Activities

There's nothing quite as effective as winter weekends for bringing out the worst in families with young kids. Here are some of our go-to cabin-fever activities. Yes, we read books and snuggle and all those wonderful things, but what about the other eleven hours of awake time?

1. Take forty-five minutes getting ready to go outside.

2. Go outside for twenty-seven seconds.

3. Go to the mall.

4. Play "Fly around and turn the lights on and off until Daddy hyperventilates."

5. Go to Best Buy and play with the refrigerators.

6. Do a puzzle for three minutes.

7. Build a fort with sofa cushions and tapestries that collapses immediately.

8. Drag the cat around on a blanket.

9. Drag a kid around on a blanket.

10. Drag both kids and the cat around on a blanket.

11. Google "symptoms of slipped disc."

12. Go to the other mall.

13. Invent games that involve lying down (see page 26).

14. Explain to the kids why it's important that they learn to play by themselves as they stare at you blankly.

15. Cover Daddy's face with duct tape.

16. Watch Mommy get duct tape out of Daddy's hair.

17. Google "wig shops in New Jersey."

18. Chase each other around until someone cries.

19. Ponder our favorite question, "What the hell is everyone else in this town DOING right now?"

20. Call all our friends and find out that they already have plans.

21. Chide ourselves for once again not making any weekend plans.

22. Play with a flashlight in the closet.

23. Explain why it hurts to get hit on the head with a flashlight.

24. Google "What's the absolute maximum amount of TV a kid can watch without developing a neurological disorder?"

Zen and the Art of Parenting

Do you ever see parents in the park or at the grocery store who seem to "just flow" with their kid's ridiculous behavior? Either they're deaf, have given up, or have learned to be a Zen parent. I'm none of those things, but if you've learned anything so far in this book, it's that I don't shy away from providing advice despite having no idea what I'm talking about. Here's how to achieve serenity.

STEP 1. Find a quiet place in your house. Right, okay, there is no quiet place in your house. In that case, go to Step 7.

STEP 2. Great, you found a quiet spot. The kids must be at school. Now sit comfortably, but not in a way that might cause you to fall asleep. If you're like me, and almost always fall asleep when you're comfortable, you should probably visit a physician because you're either depressed or suffering from sleep apnea. Remember, meditation is supposed to be a mindful but active stillness and we're not all cut out for it.

STEP 3. Cool. You made it. Now close your eyes and concentrate on your breathing. Feel the air pass in ... and ... out of your nose. If something is flapping inside your nose, or there's a slight whistling noise, let any judgment or feeling you have about it float away like a leaf in the wind. Now you're convinced the flapping thing in your nose is a leaf. Meanwhile, one of your child's toys has started beeping spontaneously. I've totally been there. You have to find a way to stop thinking about that. Now you're chanting "Stop thinking about that" over and over in your mind. You might even be singing it to the tune of the *Dora the Explorer* theme song. If so, there's really no way to make it out of this—go directly to Step 7.

STEP 4. Awesome, you're not trapped in the tautology of confusion and need caused by skipping to Step 7. Now is the time to take what you learned while meditating and spend the rest of the day "living in the moment." Remember, THERE IS NO OTHER TIME THAN THIS VERY MOMENT and now it's gone, and now that one is gone too. MOMENTS ARE DYING FASTER THAN FRUIT FLIES AND IT'S HORRIFYING HOW POWERLESS WE ARE TO STOP IT. Okay, since this attempt is only causing you to obsess about the passage of time and your own impending mortality, you're probably not ready to "live in the moment." Return to Step 1. But HURRY, it's 3 P.M. and you have to pick up your son at school in fifteen minutes. Sorry about that. I know feeling rushed is so not Zen.

STEP 5. Okay, let's say you're a placid hermit with a perfect house in the woods, the enviable ability to stop thinking about huge leaves in your nose, and you've banished the *Dora* theme song from your head (HOW?) Apparently, you can meditate without picking your nose, singing, or falling asleep. Your mind is at peace, but alert. Now look around you and appreciate how beautiful everything is and . . . uh oh, your other kid just woke up from his nap.

STEP 6. If you're here, you must not have children. Since I've never come close to getting past Step 1, this is foreign territory for me. Maybe you should paint or tend to your heirloom tomatoes.

STEP 7. Say, "Screw it, I'm just gonna eat." If you're on a diet, go to Step 7a.

STEP 7a. Buy a new house where the kids have their own wing that is insulated with soundproof foam. You'll also need a full-time nanny because, well, the kids won't really want to stay for long in this incredibly expensive soundproof area you built. If you can't afford a new house and a nanny, return to Step 7 and spend the rest of your life in an uncomfortable state of bouncing between your insatiable cravings for food and a quieter living space. If this is unappealing, go to Step 8.

STEP 8. Return to Step 1.

The Bees Are Back in Town

Remember when we were all afraid that the bees were gone forever and then we wouldn't . . . wait, what was the problem with that? Well, I found all the bees— they were hanging out at the apple orchard feasting on rotten apples and waiting for my sons. If you've never experienced a five-year-old getting a bee sting, here's what you're in for.

1. It's calm . . . beautiful.

2. The sun is shining, but the air is crisp enough to require light jackets.

3. We each have a small basket for apples.

4. This is blissful family time.

5. From the corner of your eye, you see a small arm waving back and forth.

6. You assume the child is simply fanning himself.

7. The soothing sounds of children running and the chanting of a tractor engine in the distance are suddenly and without warning, drowned out by . . .

8. BEE

9. BEE BEE

10. ## BEE BEE BEE

11. # BEE BEE BEE BEE

12. Now everyone is doing a panic dance.

13. Smaller child (to whom the bees are mysteriously unattracted) is running in circles, tripping and falling on various things.

14. Mother is swatting about furiously.

15. Father is frozen in place.

16. Older child's face now turns the color of a cartoon character holding its breath.

17. A bubble of hysteria snot peeks out of his nose, a clear sign that a sting has occurred.

18. He joins his brother in the running circle. Brother thinks it's a game and starts laughing.

19. Mother is trying to catch the victim so she can "suck out the venom."

20. Father reminds mother that the child was not bitten by a snake.

21. A crowd has assembled around the crazy family running in circles.

22. As the victim runs, two thick braids of snot swing about his head like pigtails.

23. Mother trips and almost falls, but as a result, catches the victim and screams, "WHERE DID IT STING YOU?"

24. "NECK NECK NECK!" he responds.

25. The vampire mom attempts to suck the poison from her son's neck.

26. The crowd is silent.

27. The father is silent.

28. Everyone is thinking, "Is that what you do with a bee sting?"

29. The smaller brother is still running. He trips on a pumpkin and starts crying.

30. One snot braid falls to the ground and rests gently on top of the thick orchard grass.

31. A helpful member of the audience alerts them that he would have already gone into shock by now if he were allergic to bee stings.

32. We all stare at the helpful man for a moment and he disappears into a puff of smoke.

33. A young farm hand (orchard hand?) comes by with an ointment. He's smiling and cheerfully asks, "Did someone get stung by a bee?"

34. Suddenly, we all realize that this was no big deal at all.

35. Ointment is applied, face is wiped clean, all is good.

36. Time to go home and we've been in the orchard for only twelve minutes.

37. Stop at McDonald's on the way home.

38. Spend the next year running from anything that buzzes, yelling BEE BEE BEE BEE BEE BEE BEE BEE. Assure child, "No sweetie, that's just the neighbor using his weed whacker."

39. Surprisingly, he still likes apples.

Who Needs Tissues When They Have a Sleeve?

Young children are sick for 280 days a year, but it's the secondary emotional conditions that you have to prepare for. Here are some of the syndromes you can look forward to dealing with.

ACUTE FACIAL TISSUE FEAR (AFTF)

This PTSD-related syndrome occurs when a child experiences an overly aggressive nose wipe from an adult. The child becomes completely terrified of any facial tissue, and will do almost anything to avoid contact. Methods of avoidance include screaming, running away, throwing puzzle pieces, intentionally falling face-first off the sofa, biting, slapping, spitting, etc.

COUCH SNOT SYNDROME (CSS)

This is typified by a young patient's inability to wipe his or her nose anywhere else but the sofa cushions. Generally, this is treated as a psychological problem related to AFTF, but can also be seen as a symptom of extreme fatigue and the general unwillingness to move from a comfortable position while watching *Elmo's Potty Time*.

MILK MOUTH (MM)

Also known as "webbed teeth," this is a condition caused by the excessive ingestion of milk into an already snotty mouth. The nose is clogged, so very little oxygen is introduced into the problem area. Symptoms include loud squishing noises when talking and creamy white ropes connecting the upper and lower teeth when the mouth is opened.

GAPING HACK (GH)

When a cough is coming on, the child suddenly displays an inability to turn his or her head. As a result, the contents of the cough frequently splatter on and fog the glasses of a nearby adult. In 50 percent of cases, the content enters the adult's mouth.

CRUSTED SHOULDER (CS)

Similar to CSS described previously, Crusted Shoulder is often only noticed after a parent removes his or her shirt in the evening to find they've grown snot-based papier-mâché shoulder pads (usually a result of acute CMATTS described on page 166).

OXYGEN INTAKE SWITCH SYNAPSE FAILURE (OISSF)

This is a sleeping condition seen mostly in children under three. When the nose becomes clogged, the brain fails to acknowledge its ability to take in oxygen through the mouth. Not until the patient wakes up crying from his or her inability to breathe does the mouth/nose switch synapse begin firing correctly. This is generally repeated in thirty-minute sessions throughout the night for the duration of the illness. There is no known cure, though some interesting work is being conducted at many esteemed medical research facilities.

CARRY ME ALL THE TIME SYNDROME (CMATTS)

The child refuses to be put down at all over a twelve- to thirteen-hour period. The patient is unable to extend his or her legs enough to stand or walk. They will also make horrible noises when falling anywhere beneath a parent's waistline. In extreme cases, the patient won't even permit the parent to sit down, resulting in the eventual collapse of the caretaker (COTC).

How to Make a Kid Potion

Out of what I assume was desperation, my wife taught our sons how to make "potions." These concoctions don't actually do anything—she's not a witch. A potion is simply defined as a glass full of random fluids and powders found throughout the house. Here's how they're made.

1. Get a step stool so you can reach the "nice glasses."

2. Open fridge and take out orange juice.

3. Fill glass with orange juice.

4. While carrying full glass of orange juice, kick step stool over to spice cabinet.

5. Place glass on folded kitchen towel. Make sure it's balancing precariously.

6. Get mustard powder and shake it violently over teetering glass.

7. Now go upstairs carrying full glass of orange juice and mustard powder. Spill a tiny bit with each step.

8. Open bathroom drawer. Take out eucalyptus oil and add seven to one hundred drops.

9. Grab Daddy's toothbrush, plunge it into potion and stir.

10. Pour half of contents into sink to make room for more ingredients.

11. Make sure some drips onto bath mat.

12. Add three shakes of foot powder and a handful of Epsom salts.

13. Respond to question "What are you doing up there?" with "Nothing!"

14. Find used tube of caulk. Squeeze its contents into glass. Throw empty tube in shower.

15. Stir again with toothbrush. Replace toothbrush *exactly* as you found it.

16. Now, carry glass down to kitchen. Spill accordingly.

17. Open coffeemaker and dump used contents of filter basket into glass.

18. Also while in kitchen, plop in four grapes.

19. Place glass back onto folded kitchen towel.

20. Grab a measuring cup and head down to the basement.

21. Take Daddy's favorite mug (abandon measuring cup) and scoop out some of that random fluid in bottom of vegetable drawer in basement fridge. Return to kitchen.

22. Dump half of mystery fridge liquid into glass while letting other half coat an adjacent apple.

23. Carry potion back upstairs.

24. Knock on Daddy's office door, show him the potion, and when he asks "Hey, what's in that, bud?" be honest.

25. Defibrillate Daddy.

26. Put potion on bathroom vanity; top it off with toothpaste, shaving gel, and an expired "intimate lubricant" you discovered wedged behind a box of maxi pads, and announce to whole family that no one is to touch your potion because it's "cooking."

27. Throw a fit when brother pours it into toilet and flushes.

28. Sing "Call Me Maybe" at full volume while Daddy's on the phone with plumber.

29. Announce that you now have no other choice than to make a new potion.

The Goodie Bag

Most birthday parties come with parting gifts enclosed in a festive plastic bag. That way everyone gets a present! Unfortunately, parents use these bags to punish other parents. Why? I don't know.

1. **SLIDE WHISTLE:** Why not just give the kid a siren?

2. **KAZOO:** Slightly more annoying than a slide whistle.

3. **HARMONICA:** Great! A thing that makes normal breathing sound like bagpipes.

4. **PIXY STIX:** HAVE YOU DANCED WITH THE DEVIL IN THE PALE MOONLIGHT?

5. **A YO-YO:** This is a medieval mace without the spikes.

6. **BUBBLES:** Kids insist on blowing these inside and now everything is impossibly sticky (or very clean, depending on your level of optimism).

7. **WHOOPEE CUSHION:** These break after Daddy gets a little overzealous.

8. **A LIVE GOLDFISH:** The only thing that tops a super-fun party is teaching your child the harsh realities of mortality nine hours later.

Kids Party Way Harder Than We Do

*We frequently have families over to our house—families
that have children the same age as ours. And while the
adults might have a couple beers or a few glasses of wine,
it's the kids who do the heavy partying. At the end
of the night (approximately 8 P.M.), our home looks like
a fraternity house at 6 A.M. on a Sunday.*

1. At least one kid is passed out on the sofa in the basement.

2. There's a half-eaten piece of pizza on the bookshelf.

3. Two kids leave in bare feet.

4. One kid is crying.

5. The shower is on.

6. There's a streaker.

7. The coin jar has been pillaged.

8. Two kids have to be carried out.

9. There are at least three mysterious puddles.

10. The drum set in the basement is destroyed.

11. Dozens of half-empty juice boxes are strewn about the house. One of them is stuffed in the subwoofer.

12. There's a kid in a tree.

13. One kid is wearing only a pirate hat and a pair of dress shoes.

14. EVERYTHING has been moved or placed in precarious piles.

15. Three kids are wandering around aimlessly, talking nonsense.

16. One of the toilets is broken.

17. There's a piece of plastic furniture on the lawn.

18. One kid is *still* dancing and refuses to leave.

19. Two kids are wet and won't say why.

20. Somebody puked in the hall closet.

Love Hurts:
Especially My Shoulder

Playing with and chasing around kids forces you to move your body in ways it's not meant to move, or at least in ways you haven't moved it in twenty years. Here are some of the injuries I've sustained. I can only assume they'll happen to you too.

INJURY: Inability to look to my left
LENGTH: Four days
CAUSE: Aggressive pushing of the swing

INJURY: Unspecified shoulder rotation thing
LENGTH: Ongoing
CAUSE: Per my three-year-old's request, I was trying to hit a tennis ball over the house using only a small Spider-Man paddle

INJURY: My elbow hurts (tendonitis?)
LENGTH: Permanent
CAUSE: Pulling both kids around in a clothes hamper using an extension cord as rope handle

INJURY: Tinnitus

LENGTH: Three months

CAUSE: Letting a three-year-old put a stethoscope in my ears because he promised to "only whisper" into it

INJURY: Forearm abrasions

LENGTH: Six days

CAUSE: Doing the military crawl through the tube maze at a kid's play area to rescue my emotionally frozen child

INJURY: Tender hip

LENGTH: Three months

CAUSE: Slipped playing tag on wood floors while wearing socks. This was not my fault. My son kept changing the location of the base and, well, I was about to sit down in the chair (base) when he suddenly said, "No, all the walls are bases!" I attempted a quick change of direction, my feet came out from under me, I fell, and he totally tagged me.

Of course this is all worth it because my heart is full (of cholesterol, but also love).

Dear Sons

There are many, many things I'd like to say to my kids,
but either I'm not articulate enough, too nervous,
or they're simply too young to understand them. So, I've
chosen to put a few of them in this book. I hope they will
check them out when they can read.

Dear Silas and Arlo,

1. Call me "Daddy" as long as you want. There's no pressure at all to switch to "Dad."

2. You have to stand sideways and lead with your opposite foot when you throw. Please listen to me, it's important. But since you have a great singing voice, maybe it doesn't matter.

3. You're a catch. Trust me, kid—you'll get any woman you want. Choose ones that remind you of your mom, only younger. If you choose a man, make sure he's also like your mom.

4. You inherited my skin and hair. I'm sorry.

5. I've never punched anyone in my life. Follow my lead on that; it makes you strong, not weak.

6. I'm always right. Even if I'm wrong, it's for the right reasons. Or because I'm being lazy. Or because I don't know what I'm talking about but feel like I'm supposed to. You won't understand that until you have kids of your own and that's okay.

7. I never had a brother, but always wished I did. Please get along and don't take each other for granted. If you become estranged when you're older, it will break my heart.

8. Your grandfather is the most interesting person you'll ever meet. He might not be with us for much longer. Cherish him.

9. I have attention span problems that make me unable to listen to long stories. But please don't let that discourage you from telling me long stories. I love the first few minutes of them.

10. It's possible to love someone even though they drive you insane. In fact, it might be a prerequisite.

Love,
Daddy